Cover: Lauaki Namulau'ulu Mamoe

Tumua and Pule, the orators of 'Upolu and Savai'i, the custodians of Sāmoa's customs, traditions and keepers of genealogies, had an important role in the governance of Sāmoa. Traditionally they had the role of king-makers, war-makers and peace-makers. In the 19th century Lauaki Namulau'ulu Mamoe was the leading *tulāfale* of Pule of Savai'i. He was a central figure in the struggle for political independence and advocated for Sāmoan participation in governance. His statement *'Mau a Pule'*, the opinion of Pule, would later become the motto of the Sāmoan independence movement. In March 1909, to weaken the power of Tumua and Pule, the German authorities deported Lauaki to the German colony of Saipan, in the Mariana Islands, where he died. Lauaki's voice was silenced but his message would echo down the years.

FONO

THE CONTEST FOR THE GOVERNANCE OF SĀMOA

PETER SWAIN

FOREWORD BY
TUILA'EPA DR SA'ILELE MALIELEGAOI

TE HERENGA WAKA
UNIVERSITY PRESS

Te Herenga Waka University Press
Victoria University of Wellington
PO Box 600, Wellington
New Zealand
teherengawakapress.co.nz

A catalogue record for this book is available from
the National Library of New Zealand.

ISBN 978-1-77692-065-5

Printed in Aotearoa New Zealand by Blue Star

Contents

List of Illustrations

Cover: Lauaki Namulau'ulu Mamoe

After page 100:

Seumanutafa Pogai, High Chief of Apia village, was the first point of contact for foreigners arriving in Apia harbour.

Malietoa Laupepa was a central figure in the contested governance of Sāmoa during the second half of the 19th century.

Mata'afa Iosefo was chosen to succeed Malietoa Laupepa as Sāmoa's leader, based on 'culture and tradition', and backed by Lauaki Namulau'ulu Mamoe.

Tupua Tamasese Titimaea, installed as 'King of Sāmoa' in 1887 by German political and commercial interests, backed up by German Navy gunships.

Matā'afa Iosefo, and ten of his prominent supporters, were exiled on Jaluit Atoll in the German-ruled Marshall Islands.

Tupua Tamasese Lealofi I and Solf in Berlin, where they met Kaiser Wilhelm II in 1911.

Hooray! Samoa is Ours! German poster, 1899, celebrating German governance of Sāmoa.

Constitutional Convention, 1960.

Constitutional Convention in Session: Jim Davidson, Tupua Tamasese Meaole, Malietoa Tanumafili II, Colin Aikman.

Tupua Tamasese Meaole and Malietoa Tanumafili II raising the Sāmoan flag on 1 January 1962.

Unconstitutional swearing-in ceremony, 2021.

Former Head of State at the unconstitutional swearing-in ceremony.

Police blockade of HRPP MPs from Parliament.

Tuila'epa addresses crowd outside Parliament.

The Chief Justice and members of the Judiciary, accompanied by Police, head to Parliament Buildings.

Tuila'epa leads HRPP MPs into Parliament to be sworn in.

Foreword

Talofa lava.

Fono – The Contest for the Governance of Sāmoa is essential reading for all Sāmoans, and for all those interested in the good governance of small island states. This book, based on a wide range of historical sources and original research, provides us with fresh insights into the history of Sāmoa and the struggles our leaders and people went through in their search for the ideal form of governance for Sāmoans to live their own way of life. The hard-fought 2021 contest for the governance of Sāmoa is also discussed in detail.

Sāmoa, a former colony of Germany, was administered by New Zealand from 1914 under a mandate by the League of Nations and later as a Territory under a United Nations Trusteeship. Following the breakup of the British, French, German, Japanese, Italian, Dutch and Portuguese empires after World War II, the process of decolonisation began. Many countries in Africa, Asia, the Caribbean and the Pacific were in a similar political situation to Sāmoa, waiting for United Nations clearance to run their own affairs. The United Nations was not in a hurry and gave priority to the state of preparedness and the assured majority support of the citizens for independence of a state to be secured through democratic processes and not through coercion. This took time. The United Nations did not want to see any new states fail. Peace at all costs, following the two world wars, was the uttermost consideration in the minds of world leaders of the newly formed United Nations.

Sāmoan leaders' persistence for independent status, supported by the New Zealand Government's assurances of Sāmoa's readiness for self-government, eventually convinced the United Nations to grant Sāmoa independence as a special test case. If Sāmoa proved successful, other Trust Territories would be considered for similar treatment. Fiji received its independence in 1970, followed by Papua New Guinea in 1975 and then other new Pacific Island nations followed suit.

On 1 January 1962 Sāmoa celebrated its independence. 'The Independent State of Western Sāmoa' was renamed in a 1997 constitutional amendment as 'The Independent State of Sāmoa'. The name change deleted the final sign of foreign governance imposed by force, which had resulted in divisions and conflict amongst our people over two centuries. Independence brought to an end the contest for the governance of Sāmoa by foreign powers. The contest for governance then shifted to indigenous Sāmoan political leaders, soon to be expressed through competing party politics.

Chapter Six of this volume captures the essence of the contest between the two major political parties in the 2021 General Election: The Human Rights Protection Party (HRPP) and the newly formed Faʻatuatua i le Atua Sāmoa ua Tasi (FAST) Party. The leaders of FAST were Fiamē Naomi Matāʻafa, former Deputy Prime Minister, who resigned from my cabinet in the lead up to the 2021 General Election, and Laauli Schmidt, former Speaker and cabinet minister in the 2011–2016 HRPP Government, who was forced to resign as Minister of Agriculture in 2018.

Their main complaint centred on three Constitutional Amendment Bills tabled in Parliament following cabinet deliberations spanning several months. Consultation on the bills with all the districts of Sāmoa was carried out by the Bills Committee of Parliament over a period of six months before the final passing into law by Parliament on 15 December 2020. This was the culmination of years of dedicated work by a Special Committee of Parliament, established in early 2016, assisted by a team of lawyers from the Attorney General's Office and the Office of the Law Review Commission, to examine, discuss and recommend to Parliament appropriate legislative reforms to strengthen the judiciary's institutional capacity.

The three Constitutional Amendment Bills aimed to reflect the view of the Founding Fathers of the Constitution that both individual and communal rights should be accorded recognition in Sāmoa's Constitution. The Late Chief Justice, Patu Falefatu Sapolu, used the term 'Legal Pluralism' to refer to a country with two legal systems. The role of the Chiefs and Orators, in the maintenance of law and order in the community in relation to any disputes on claims to chiefly titles and customary land usages, continues to be addressed by the Land and Titles Court and is now formally incorporated into the Constitution, in the same way as the Civil Courts deal with civil and criminal matters.

Chief Justice Patu had stressed the importance of these constitutional reforms in order for our customary practices and traditions to be fully recognised in our Constitution, the highest law of the land. He said to me, 'I shed tears many times when giving judgement on a dispute involving individual rights versus communal rights of the chiefs and orators affected. With only individual rights protected by the Constitution, the rights of our leaders in the community must always receive an unavoidable TKO (technical knockout).' It took five years of careful review, from the first discussion in Parliament and establishing the Special Parliamentary Committee, to begin the review of the three Constitutional Amendment Bills, from early 2016 to final approval on 15 December 2020.

The judiciary, through Chief Justice Patu and the President of the Land and Titles Court, Fepuleai Atila, provided valuable input into the three bills. I believe that the constitutional amendments were politicised during the 2021 General Election and their constitutional significance will only be fully appreciated when the excitement of the politics around the General Election dies down and Sāmoa settles down to business as usual.

Great lessons have been learnt. The reason why this book is important for all Sāmoans is that it is published at an opportune moment when recent events in our political history are fresh in our minds. Recent events have tested the principle of the separation of powers. It is critical in small democracies, where the extended family system presents a huge challenge, to ensure the independence of the three branches of government through the rigid observance of constitutionally established checks and balances on power.

Clear guidelines are in place to protect the judiciary against allegations of lack of independence. Judges from similar jurisdictions, like Tonga, Fiji and Papua New Guinea, can be engaged to rule on highly sensitive electoral-related litigation. We must remember that no one is above the law, that justice delayed is justice denied, and that positive action must be seen to be done in the delivery of justice. These principles are particularly important when the judiciary is called on to rule on controversial, political matters.

True separation of powers is extremely important for the proper functioning of our democracy. Power by its very nature tends to corrupt. Hence the dictum: power corrupts and absolute power corrupts absolutely. The solution to this conundrum is to use power to balance power. The very reason power is given to one branch of government is to provide an effective check and balance against the abuse of power by another branch.

That is the reason why our Chief Justice and President of the Land and Titles Court are appointed by the Head of State, on the advice of the Prime Minister. And the Chief Justice and President of the Land and Title Court can only be removed by Parliament with a two-thirds majority vote. The judiciary's function is to interpret the law passed by Parliament, the supreme law-making body of the land.

Sāmoa is a Christian nation with culture and traditions kept alive by the custodians of our *fa'asāmoa,* the prominent orator class Tumua and Pule. Sāmoa remains a peaceful nation. Despite a prolonged political impasse during 2021, we were able to negotiate a peaceful outcome which truly reflects the maturity and tolerance nurtured by the living culture and the deep Christian values of our Sāmoan people.

Sixty years of independent governance has led to a good level of political maturity in Sāmoa, demonstrating a powerful sense of tolerance by the leaders of the people. The HRPP's peaceful disputation of the 2021 electoral result led to unnecessary fears of lawlessness. That never happened. It is good to be reminded of the wisdom of old expressed in the Sāmoan proverb: *E tetele a Pesega ae matua lava ile oō.* Regardless of how great our differences are, a peaceful resolution is always achievable.

We have a government now facing numerous challenges, and we, the Leader and Members of the Human Rights Protection Party, give all our support to the FAST Government as is the norm for any Opposition party. The time for politics is over. It is now the time for nation building. As a democratic Opposition party we remain loyal to our Constitution and committed to the good governance of the Independent State of Sāmoa.

'Ia manuia

Tuila'epa Dr Sa'ilele Malielegaoi

Preface

If you know your history, then you would know where you're coming from[1]

During the time Prime Minister Tuila'epa Sa'ilele Malielegaoi and I were writing his memoir, *Pālemia,* we came to understand that it was necessary to place his story in the context of Sāmoa's political development since independence. We also aimed to make that history factual and easy to read.

Sāmoa has a very long and interesting history. But that history is often recorded in obscure academic texts that are hard to find and read, written from a particular, personal point of view, or stored away in the minds of our elders. Following the publication of *Pālemia* many people talked with me about the history of Sāmoa. They showed great interest and told me they had enjoyed reading Sāmoan history but had either 'forgotten', or did not know of, the specific events that we had written about in *Pālemia*.

There is a thirst for more accessible stories about Sāmoan political history and so I set about researching and writing the story of the contest for the governance of Sāmoa from first settlement up to the present day. The events of the 2021 General Election provided a fitting conclusion to this narrative.

All history is contestable. Sāmoa's written history has been a contest between those who aim to justify past actions and those who seek to establish an objective historical record. I have aimed to tell a balanced history that sets out the story of the development of Sāmoa's unique system of governance, highlight its roots in the *fa'asāmoa* and the *fa'amatai,* and identify the events that have shaped that history and the people who have contested for Sāmoa's governance.

Fa'afetai tele lava lau Afioga Tuila'epa Sa'ilele Malielegaoi. Tuila'epa read my manuscript, made suggestions for improvements, contributed notes on constitutional amendments and women's parliamentary

1   From the lyrics of 'Buffalo Soldier', by Bob Marley and Noel Williams.

representation (see Appendix 2) and generously wrote the Foreword. The responsibility for the text is mine alone, including any errors, oversights, omissions or opinions.

I acknowledge and thank the team at Te Herenga Waka University Press: Fergus Barrowman, Publisher and the production team. Fa'afetai tele lava Galumalemana Alfereti Hunkin for proofreading and Atoese Morgan Tuimalealiifano for reading the manuscript. Luamanuvao Dame Winnie Laban has been an inspiration and my partner on this and our other Pacific journeys together. *Alofa atu.*

It is hoped that *Fono – The Contest for the Governance of Sāmoa* will stimulate interest and inform debate about the governance of Sāmoa.

'Ia manuia lava
Peter Swain

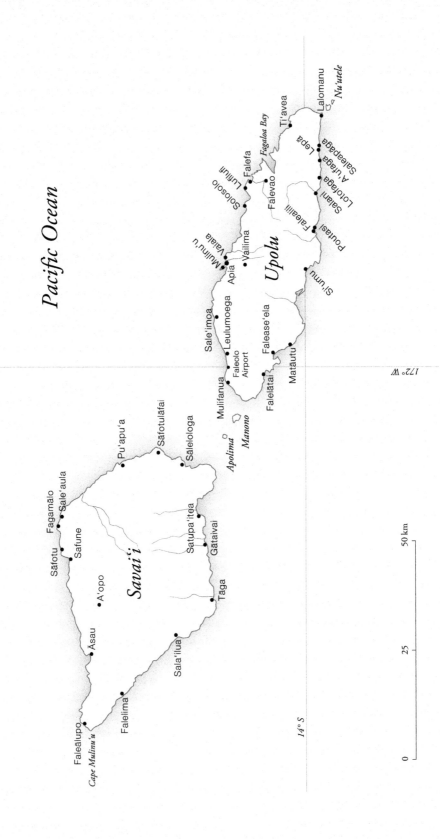

Pacific Ocean

Savai'i

Cape Mulinu'u
Falealupo
Falelima
Sala'ilua
Āsau
A'opo
Safotu
Fagamālo
Sale'aula
Safune
Pu'apu'a
Sāfotulāfai
Sālelologa
Satupa'itea
Gātaivai
Tāga

Apolima
Manono

Mulifanua
Faleolo Airport
Sale'imoa
Leulumoega
Falease'ela
Falelātai
Matāutu

Mulinu'u
Vaiala
Vailima
Apia

Solosolo
Lufilufi
Falefa
Fagaloa Bay
Falevao

Upolu

Faleali'i
Poutasi
Salani
Lotofaga
A'ufaga
Lepā
Saleapaga
Si'umu
Ti'avea
Lalomanu
Nu'utele

14° S

0   25   50 km

172° W

Prologue

Fono – The Contest for the Governance of Sāmoa *tells the story of the development of Sāmoa's unique system of governance and those who have fought for power and shaped the development of the Independent State of Sāmoa.*

From a Tribal Society to a Modern State

There has been continuous inhabitation of the Sāmoan islands for around 3,000 years, much of that time without contact from outside the Polynesian universe.[1] During those millennia the people settled into independent, self-governing village communities and developed democratic[2] governance structures and processes to manage the day-to-day administration of the community, its land and natural resources.[3]

Governance was centred on a *fono,*[4] a village council comprised of *matai*, the chosen heads of families and extended families, *'āiga, 'āigapotopoto*. A *fa'alupega* set out the names and titles of the *matai*, their order of precedence, historical associations and relationships. Village *fono* directed the affairs of the village and exercised sacred authority. Meetings of the *fono* are still held regularly, usually in the

1   Meleisea, 1995: 20, tells us that Sāmoans conceive of four distinct periods of the past: 1. Prehistoric time from Creation to Tongan domination; 2. The time of Tongan domination (12–15th century); 3. The time of the Tafa'ifā, to around the end of the 19th century; and 4. The time when Christianity was introduced in 1830 to the present day.
2   Democracy is a system of governance by the whole population through elected representatives. Sāmoan chiefs, *matai*, are elected heads of extended families and represent the views of their family at village *fono*.
3   Communalism is the dictionary definition and label applied by political scientists to self-governing communities.
4   In Sāmoan, the word *fono* is both a noun and a verb, referring to the village council, a legislative assembly, a committee, meeting, conference, rally or similar event, and to the act of holding a meeting. *Fono* has other meanings: the plank of a canoe, to mend, to fill, to plug or patch, or to provide food to accompany kava. (Milner, 1966, Pratt, 1977.)

faletele, meeting house, of the senior *matai.* After a formal welcome, acknowledging each *matai* and the purpose of the *fono,* matters requiring decisions are debated until unanimity is reached. Refined over centuries of practice, village government by *fono* combines flexibility and stability. Consensus decision-making by *matai* moderates and counteracts the accumulation of individual personal power. *Fono* are an indigenous form of localised, democratic governance – by the people for the people. When Robert Louis Stephenson first encountered Sāmoan *fono* in the 1890s he wrote, 'We have passed the feudal system; they are not yet clear of the patriarchal. We are thick in the age of finance; they are in a period of communism.'[5]

Villages formed alliances with nearby villages for security, or other mutual benefits. These relationships were often cemented by arranged marriages; men married women from outside of their own village. Over time, deep and complex familial relationships developed; these were recorded and memorised in *faʻalupega* and *gafa,* genealogies.

The structure of larger political units, sub-districts *faigāmālō,* districts *itūmālō,* and all of Sāmoa, echoed the principles of the village structure in that each had a *faʻalupega* and *fono,* but their functions were different. The necessities of day-to-day administration were in the control of village *fono.* At the national level lineage interests were important and there was often tension and competition for succession to major titles, including the *Tafaʻifā.*[6] Warfare often ensued when *fono* were unable to resolve contests between districts for paramount *matai* titles. Sāmoa was essentially a tribal society in which 'contested lineage interests effectively prevented the growth of a strong and stable central government'.[7] [8] Furthermore, the Sāmoans did not face

5   Stevenson, 1892: 1–2. Stevenson uses the word 'communism' in the pure
    sense of meaning a self-governing community. Stevenson knew of the French
    Communards of the 18th century, but it is unlikely that he was aware of the
    political system that would later be known as Communism. The Communist
    Manifesto was published in German in 1848 by Marx and Engels.
6   See Appendix 1 for lists of *Tama-a-ʻĀiga* lineages, paramount titles, from the
    19th century to the present day.
7   See Davidson, 1967: 30.
8   Soʻo, 2008: 10, notes that the *Tafaʻifā* was '. . . the closest political framework
    Sāmoa had to that of a central government as it is understood in the modern

any significant threats from outside that would provide a reason for districts to join forces and form a national government to repel an invader.

The Sāmoan Islands were rich in natural resources. Subsistence was relatively easy, food was plentiful, and village communities had the time and leisure to develop rich cultural, social and religious practices. Apart from the occasional natural disaster, wrought by extreme weather events, volcanic eruptions or earthquakes and infrequent warfare, the living was easy.

For a thousand years after its foundation, the Polynesian universe, Oceania, remained confined to a handful of islands centred on Sāmoa and Tonga. Two periods of disruption unsettled the calm. The first disruption came around 1,000 BCE when there was a period of Polynesian exploration and expansion[9] leading to the settlement of the Polynesian Triangle: Hawai'i in the north, Rapanui to the east, Aotearoa in the south and all the islands in between, including the establishment of trade networks within Polynesia.[10] Epeli Hau'ofa[11] described Oceania as: '. . . a large world in which people and cultures moved and mingled, unhindered by boundaries of the kind erected much later by imperial powers. From one island to another they sailed to trade and to marry, thereby expanding social networks for greater flows of wealth. They travelled to visit relatives in a wide variety of natural and cultural surroundings, to quench their thirst for adventure, and even to fight and dominate.'

The second disruption came when Europeans, *papālagi* cloud-bursters, shattered the calm of the Pacific. In the 17th and 18th

sense.'

9   Perhaps the impetus to leave was population growth, the thwarted ambition of younger brothers, or a changing climate that made distant travel easier or imperative? Whatever the reason, this was a period of disruption. Participants of the Polynesian diaspora took elements of the systems of governance of their homelands with them, and when they settled systems of governance evolved to suit the new situation.

10 Andrew Crowe, 2018: 231. Crowe's *Pathway of the Birds* maps the extensive pre-European trade networks within Polynesia. The islands of Melanesia and Micronesia also had extensive trade networks.

11 Hau'ofa, 1994: 153–4.

centuries explorers and adventurers entered Polynesia. Then, in the 19th century, traders, missionaries and settlers followed, seeking land for agriculture, commerce and settlement. European powers competing for territory, resources and political influence fought over the governance of Sāmoa.

The Germans, French, Americans and British each sought political advantage by promoting and backing various individual leaders for the role of 'King of Sāmoa'. The Europeans lacked an understanding of the wisdom of the democratic nature of the communal, indigenous leadership of Sāmoa, and each promoted their chosen 'King' as sole ruler. And the occasional ambitious Sāmoan leader was seduced by the lure of supreme office. The foreign intervention into the political affairs of Sāmoa was not welcomed and led to a period of increased disruption, conflict and civil strife. Over time, the chiefs of Sāmoa lost their political power as the outsiders gained control.

In 1900 the island group was split and Germany assumed full political control of 'German' (Western) Sāmoa, and the United States of America took control of 'American' (Eastern) Sāmoa. In 1914 a New Zealand Expeditionary Force invaded and took possession of German Sāmoa. After the end of World War I, New Zealand administered Western Sāmoa under a Mandate from the League of Nations. From 1945 Western Sāmoa became a Trust Territory of the United Nations, administered by New Zealand, until it achieved independence in 1962. American Sāmoa remains an unincorporated territory of the United States of America.

Sixty years after losing political independence, and indigenous sovereignty, Western Sāmoa was established as an independent Westminster-style parliamentary democracy with *matai* suffrage. In 1991 universal suffrage was established. Sovereignty was further asserted when 'Western' was dropped from Sāmoa's name in 1997, and again in 2014 when the two remaining 'European/Individual' seats in Parliament were abolished. By 2016 the Independent State of Sāmoa had returned to governance by a 'Parliament of Chiefs'.

The political development of a nation state tends to follow a universal pattern, but each state has some unique particulars. The establishment of a state, the introduction of the rule of law and the formalisation of mechanisms of accountability are three common elements of political order that the Independent State of Sāmoa has put in place. Francis Fukuyama tells us that state institutions '. . . concentrate power and allow the community to deploy that power to enforce laws, keep the peace, defend itself against outside enemies and provide necessary public goods.' The rule of law, and mechanisms of accountability, by contrast '. . . constrain the state's power and ensure that it is used only in a controlled and consensual manner.' Fukuyama says that 'the miracle of modern politics is that we can have political orders that are simultaneous strong and capable and yet constrained to act only within the parameters established by law and democratic choice.'[12]

Successful states find ways and means to manage the tension between state power and the rule of law through mechanisms of accountability. For a healthy democracy the separation of powers between the legislature, the executive and the judiciary is necessary.

Sāmoa's political development has followed a path that is common for many newly independent nations; however, because of its history and cultural heritage, there are some aspects of Sāmoa's political development that are unique. For example, Sāmoa has: built a pluralist legal system that supports the modern ideal of democracy and individual human rights without significantly compromising its communal cultural heritage; established a Land and Titles Court, with Sāmoan judges, *fa'amasino,* to deal with disputes over customary lands and titles; requires *matai* status for eligibility to stand for Parliament; and has developed an independent judiciary comprised of qualified, professional Sāmoan judges.[13]

There has been a tension throughout the history of Sāmoa's political development between the move towards establishing a modern, independent, democratic state, with institutions that provide checks and balances on individual power, and traditional governance based on communal, familial and kin relationships. This tension has been exacerbated by the small size, connectedness and intimacy of

12 Fukuyama, 2014: 24–25.
13 Sāmoa's pluralist legal system is still evolving. See discussion in Chapter 6.

Sāmoa's population. In *The Origins of Political Order*, Fukuyama puts his finger on the problem: 'Once states come into being, kinship becomes an obstacle to political development, since it threatens to return political relationships to the small-scale, personal ties of tribal societies.'

Fono – The Contest for the Governance of Sāmoa aims to tell a balanced story of Sāmoa's political journey from an isolated 'tribal society'[14] to a globally connected, modern, independent, democratic state where the strengths of tradition, *fa'asāmoa* and the *fa'amatai,* have been harnessed to support the political development and governance of the nation state.

---

14 Fukuyama, 2012: 81, tells us that state-level societies differ from tribal societies because: they possess a centralised source of authority (Monarch, President, Prime Minister); the authority of the state is backed by a monopoly of the legitimate form of authority (police, army); the state is territorial rather than kin-based; states are more stratified and unequal than tribal societies; and states are often legitimised by religious belief. The Independent State of Sāmoa meets these criteria.

Chapter 1

Sāmoa's Parliament of Chiefs

The Pacific Islands were the last places on Earth to be settled by humankind. Some four thousand years ago the ancestors of today's Sāmoans sailed east and settled remote Oceania. In the Sāmoan Islands they developed a complex culture and a unique form of governance – a parliament of chiefs.

First Settlement

Up to ten thousand years ago people had been able to walk from place to place or use simple boats to find new lands; until they came across the Pacific Ocean, the largest geographical feature of the Earth. The blue Pacific covers a third of the surface of the planet. The development of new technologies – long-range ocean voyaging by canoe with reliable navigation systems – was necessary to voyage across the ocean and to reach the Pacific Islands.[1] Archaeological evidence shows us that the Proto-Polynesians, the people who became Polynesians, also known as the Lapita people, arrived by sea from the west establishing foundation populations in Sāmoa and Tonga. It was in the Sāmoan Islands that these ancestors became Sāmoan.[2]

1   See: *We, the Navigators: The Ancient Art of Landfinding in the Pacific,* by David Lewis.
2   There is an extensive and growing literature on the settlement of the Pacific Islands, see: *Vaka Moana, Voyages of the Ancestors – The Discovery and Settlement of the Pacific,* edited by K. Rowe, and *Pathway of the Birds: The voyaging achievements of Māori and their Polynesian ancestors,* by Andrew Crowe, for accessible overviews of the settlement of the Pacific. *Vaka Moana* outlines current research and writing on archaeological, linguistic and biological evidence of Polynesian migration and settlement, and *Pathway*

Moana was the common name for these native seas, now called the Pacific Ocean. Vast voyaging networks connected the islands of Polynesia, Melanesia and Micronesia. *'O le Vasa Loloa* linked Sāmoa with Tonga, Fiji, Rotuma, Futuna and Uvea. *Moana-nui-a Kiwa* linked Eastern Polynesia south to Aotearoa.[3] *Hira, Kula* and the Vitiaz Strait route are trade networks linking islands and coastal regions of Papua New Guinea. The Santa Cruz Islands, the Western Solomon Islands, Yap and the Caroline islands also had extensive reciprocal trade networks.[4]

Archaeological, linguistic and biological evidence (DNA) supports recent scientific explanations of the history of Polynesian voyaging and the settlement of the Pacific Islands.[5] To explain the development of the governance of Sāmoa, we need to look to human sources, including oral traditions.[6]

Origin Stories

Polynesian oral tradition provides a number of origin stories.[7] Tagaloa-a-lagi, the Polynesian God, is a common figure in these stories and

of the Birds identifies prehistoric trading routes within Polynesia. J. Robert Shaffer's *Sāmoa: A Historical Novel* gives a fictional account of the settlement of Sāmoa based on historical evidence.

3   See Damon Salesa, 2013, 2018, for recent research on Polynesian voyaging networks. There were similar voyaging and trading networks in Melanesia and Micronesia.

4   I have drawn extensively on Davidson (1967), Gilson (1970), Kramer (1901, 1994), Meleisea (1987), So'o (2008), Turner (1884, 1984) and others for accounts of the development of Sāmoa's traditional polity.

5   See Howe, 2006: 200–245.

6   A recent study of the Sāmoan genome indicates that the small founding population expanded around 1,000 years ago. See Harris et al., 2020. 'Evolutionary History of Modern Sāmoans'.

7   Oral histories are often contested and contradictory. Some stories are mythical and legendary and need to be treated with caution. Rawiri Taonui provides a good summary of Polynesian oral traditions in *Vaka Moana*, 2006: 24–53. The origin stories presented here are extracted from Kramer, an Ethnologist, and Turner, a Missionary, who gathered their material from Sāmoans in the late 19th century and from the diaries, logbooks and other accounts of early explorers.

Manu'a Island a common location. The distinction between 'gods' and 'men' has been blurred by time. Some stories have the Tui Manu'a, a descendant of the god Tagaloa-a-lagi as the first settler. In one story Tagaloa-a-lagi is said to have entered Sāmoa (and Tonga) from the east (perhaps from Manu'a). Another story tells us that Tagaloa's son Pili had three sons: the twins, Tua and Ana, and Saga. From these the three political districts of 'Upolu are derived: Tua founded the political district Ātua (that of Tua), the eastern third of 'Upolu; Ana founded Ā'ana, the western third of 'Upolu; and Saga founded Tuamāsaga (after the twins), the district between Ātua and Ā'ana.[8] Another story adds a fourth brother, Tolufale, who went to and founded the political districts of Savai'i, and tells of the wars between the brothers.[9] [10]

Chiefly Titles

Today's paramount chiefly titles, the *ali'i* of Sāmoa, are derived from legendary and pre-historic figures. The paramount chiefly titles Tui Ātua and Tui Ā'ana appear to be among the oldest in Sāmoa and the first Tui Ātua was said to be Leutelele'i'ite who lived around 1170AD.[11] Around the 12th century the Mālietoa title was also established and became the paramount title of the Tuamāsaga district. The political divisions of Savai'i can be traced to several oral traditions. Fune, a great and feared warrior (Funefe'ai, Fune the Savage), established a number of villages in Savai'i. His *tulāfale* (orator chiefs) were known as Sā Fune (the family of Fune). Around the 10th century Fune took the title Le Tagaloa. Another Savai'i title, Tonumaipe'a, has links with the Tui Tonga[12] and was established around the 12th century,

8   See So'o, 2008: 4–9, also Meleisea, 1987: 1–20.
9   See 'The Story of the War of the Brothers' in Kramer, Vol.1, 1994: 30.
10 Tuila'epa asserts that the 'correct version recognised by all the orators of Sāmoa' is that Pili had four sons: Ātua, Ā'ana, Saga and Tolufale.
11 So'o, 2008: 2.
12 Meleisea, 1995: 20, refers to the time of Tongan domination of Sāmoa, for perhaps 300 years, that ended around the 15th century. The influence of the Tui Tonga, the King of Tonga, from that time can still be identified in the names of some *matai* titles, eg: Malietoa, Lauaki, Tuila'epa.

and the Lilomaiava title was established in the 15th century. Though established independently, these ancient Savai'i titles have linkages, through marriages and alliances, with the three paramount titles from 'Upolu.

The details of ancient Sāmoan chiefly titles are obscured in the mists of time and are subject to debate by historians, researchers and today's descendants of these ancient lineages. Oral histories are not always reliable and are subject to bias and inaccuracies due to faulty or selective memories. Today, we have access to written records from the 19th century of *gafa* recorded in *fa'alupega* and memorised by *tulāfale*. These records, while often contested, are used by the Judges of Sāmoa's Land and Titles Court as evidence to settle lineage disputes.

Four paramount titles that emerged in the 16th century are known as the *pāpā* titles. These *ali'i* titles were all acquired by the Tonumaipe'a *'āiga* (family network) in the 15th century, following a series of wars, and were later conferred upon Salamasina, a female descendant of the Tui Tonga. On the rare occasions when the four *pāpā* titles have been conferred on one person they are referred to as the *Tafa'ifā* (literally: four-in-one). Two of the *pāpā* titles were Tui Ātua and Tui Ā'ana and the other two were named after Salamasina's grandmother Vaeotamasolali'i and Vaeotamasolali'i's aunt Gato'aitele. Vaeotamasolali'i and Gato'aitele were direct descendants of Malietoa La'auli.

The ancient *pāpā* titles are reflected in the paramount titles of modern Sāmoa: Malietoa, Tupua, Matā'afa and Tuimaleali'ifano. The holders of these paramount titles are often referred to as *tama-a-'āiga*[13] (sons of the *'āiga*).

When *pāpā* titles become vacant, *'āiga* organise to select and promote their preferred candidate. These networks of kin, descended from a common ancestor, are vast and complex and can involve whole districts. So'o[14] writes that these *'āiga* alliances '. . . may be considered as the traditional equivalent of modern-day political parties . . . and still influence Sāmoan political thinking and traditional attitudes to

13 See Tuimaleali'ifano, 2006 for a detailed history on the origin of the *tama-a-*
    'āiga and an analysis of the politics of succession to Sāmoa's paramount titles.
14 So'o, 2008: 211–215.

politics.' Holders of Sāmoan *matai* titles can trace an historical link directly, or through marriage, to one or more *'āiga*, maximal lineages or political families, established before European contact including: 'Āiga Sa Levālasi, 'Āiga Sa Tuala, 'Āiga Sa Fenunu'ivao, 'Āiga Sa Tunumafono, 'Āiga Sa Taulagi, 'Āiga Sa Moelēoi, 'Āiga Sa Pesetā, 'Āiga Sa 'Amituana'i, 'Āiga Sa Tago.

Governance

Supreme political authority (sovereignty, power) in Sāmoa is not held alone by a paramount chief. Sāmoa's indigenous governance is collective and communal. At the village, district or national level political power is negotiated and balanced between *ali'i* and *tulāfale*. An *ali'i* may hold a paramount title, but the right to bestow that title may rest with groups of *tulāfale*. For example: nine orator families, *faleiva*, of Ā'ana have the right to confer the Tui Ā'ana title, and six orator families, *faleono*, of Lufilufi have the right to confer the Tui Ātua title. Sharing the conferring of power is one of the ways that checks and balances on political authority are built into the processes of the *fa'asāmoa*.

Tūmua and *Pule* are the traditional political centres of 'Upolu and Savai'i. These both have legendary origins and modern-day manifestations. The original centres of *Tūmua* were at Lufulufi in Ātua and Leulumoega in Ā'ana and refer to groups of *tulāfale*, the *fale'upolu*, who met in those places. Malie and Afega later became political centres of *Tūmua* on 'Upolu. The villages of Sāfotulāfai and Sāle'aula were the original centres of *Pule* in Savai'i. Sātupa'itea, Āsau, Vailoa and Sāfotu later gained *Pule* status in the 19th century.

Villages were, and remain, the basic unit of political organisation in Sāmoa. At the village government level, various factors interacted to create a system that combined flexibility and stability. Personal power was moderated and counteracted by the changing balance within the lineage structure. At the national level, where lineage interests were far more important and the necessities of day-to-day administration were wholly absent, they effectively prevented the growth of a strong and stable central government.[15]

When two or more adjacent villages joined together, for security or mutual assistance, they were known as *faigāmālō*, and when several *faigāmālō* agreed to combine in a political arrangement or for warfare under a paramount title, an *itūmālō* was established. Eleven *itūmālō* comprise today's political districts: Fa'asālele'aga, Gāgā'emauga, Gāgāifomauga, Vaisigano, Satupa'itea and Palauli on Savai'i and Tuamāsaga, Ā'ana, 'Āiga i le Tai (including Apolima and Manono Islands), Ātua and Va'a o Fonoti on 'Upolu. (See map) The boundaries of today's parliamentary electorates are influenced by the traditional areas of the *itūmālō*, along with population numbers and demographic factors.

Most authorities agree that Sāmoa did not have a central government in the centuries before European contact. In the 19th century George Turner noted: 'A hurried glance, from a European stand-point, has caused many passing visitors to conclude that the Sāmoans have nothing whatsoever in the shape of government or laws.'[16] Sāmoan governance could be described as communalism, rule by self-governing communities, a parliament of chiefs. In the early 19th century, European powers were monarchies or aristocracies, ruled by kings or nobles, and just entering the early stages of their development as democracies. Turner reflected that, 'A good deal of order was maintained by the union of two things, viz. *civil power* and *superstitious fear*.' '[Sāmoan] government had, and still has, more of the patriarchal and democratic in it than the monarchical.' More recently, Morgan Tuimaleali'ifano[17] noted that 'Power [in Sāmoa] was derived from the sacred authority associated with ancestry [rather] than from the secular authority associated with Western notions of monarchy'. A misreading by Europeans of the nature of indigenous Sāmoan governance was at the heart of many of the conflicts over the following hundred years. European powers attempted to fill a perceived leadership void during the 19th century by attempting to create a central government through promoting one or other of the

15 Davidson, 1967: 30.
16 Turner, 1884: 173.
17 Tuimaleali'ifano, 2006: 4.

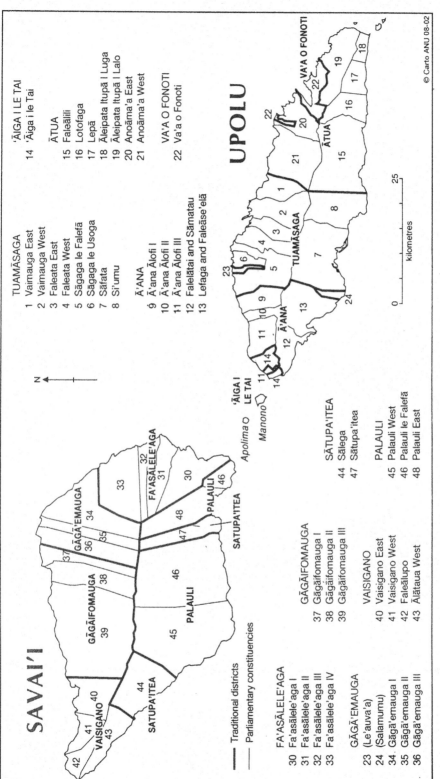

TUAMĀSAGA
1 Vaimauga East
2 Vaimauga West
3 Faleata East
4 Faleata West
5 Sāgaga le Falefā
6 Sāgaga le Usoga
7 Sāfata
8 Si'umu

Ā'ANA
9 Ā'ana Ālofi I
10 Ā'ana Ālofi II
11 Ā'ana Ālofi III
12 Falelātai and Sāmatau
13 Lefaga and Faleāse'elā

'ĀIGA I LE TAI
14 'Āiga i le Tai

ĀTUA
15 Faleā:ili
16 Lotofaga
17 Lepā
18 Āleipata Itupā I Luga
19 Āleipata Itupā I Lalo
20 Anoāma'a East
21 Anoāma'a West

VA'A O FONOTI
22 Va'a o Fonoti

N

UPOLU

© Carto ANU 08-02

kilometres
0   25

FA'ASĀLELE'AGA
30 Fa'asālele'aga I
31 Fa'asālele'aga II
32 Fa'asālele'aga III
33 Fa'asālele'aga IV

GĀGĀ'EMAUGA
23 (Le'auva'a)
24 (Salamumu)
34 Gāgā'emauga I
35 Gāgā'emauga II
36 Gāgā'emauga III

GĀGĀIFOMAUGA
37 Gāgāifomauga I
38 Gāgāifomauga II
39 Gāgāifomauga III

VAISIGANO
40 Vaisigano East
41 Vaisigano West
42 Faleālupo
43 Ālātaua West

SĀTUPA'ITEA
44 Sālega
47 Sātupa'itea

PALAULI
45 Palauli West
46 Palauli le Falefā
48 Palauli East

— Traditional districts
— Parliamentary constituencies

Sāmoa's Political Districts (Asofou Soʻo, *Democracy & Custom in Samoa*, USP, 2008)

paramount chiefs to the role of 'King of Sāmoa'.

Ancient chiefly titles and political institutions that can be traced back to the remote past still have an influence on the governance of Sāmoa in the 21st century. And narratives of Sāmoan history and traditions are often contested and conflicting. Tuimaleali'ifano asserts[18] 'the Sāmoan past is malleable and vulnerable to constant reinvention to suit the political present'. If we are to understand the governance of Sāmoa today, we need to have a good knowledge of historical rivalries, the shape of Sāmoan political organisation and its collective, communal decision-making, and the *gafa* of those involved, because the tensions, rivalries and challenges of the past are with us in the present and will surely influence the future governance of Sāmoa.

18 Tuimaleali'ifano, 2006: 85.

Chapter 2

European Contact, Settlement and Governance

Europeans first made contact with Sāmoans early in the 18th century. They found a society based on village governance. During the 19th century the European 'great powers' competed with each other, and Sāmoans, for national control. By the end of the 19th century Germany ruled Sāmoa.

European Explorers

Three millennia of Polynesian isolation were shattered when Europeans, *papālagi*,[1] arrived in Sāmoa.[2] Jacob Roggeveen, Louis-Antoine de Bougainville and Jean-François de Galaup, Compte de La Pérouse were the first Europeans to make contact with Sāmoans.[3]

In 1722 Jacob Roggeveen,[4] leading an expedition sponsored by the Dutch West India Company, entered the Pacific with the aim of opening a western trade route to the Spice Islands, today's Indonesia.

---

1   Prior to Roggeveen's visit Sāmoans had heard of *papālagi*, and received some glass beads, from Tongans who had earlier received visitors from Europe in 1616 and 1643. This is clear evidence that there was extensive pre-European contact between Sāmoa, Tonga and Fiji. See: Kramer, Vol. II, 1995: 6; Teherkézoff, 2008: 19.

2   Tongans, and other Polynesians from the Eastern Lau Group of Fiji and Uvea, visited Sāmoa. There was warfare and intermarriage between the chiefly families as evidenced in the titles Kamasese/Tamasese, Tulakepa/Tuila'epa. The Malietoa title's origin comes from the final words of the Tongan warriors as they were fleeing from Sāmoa: 'Malie To'a, Malo e tau . . .' ('Great warrior, thank you for the war').

3   Captain James Cook, the most active explorer of the Pacific in the 17th century, never visited the Sāmoan Islands, or Fiji, in spite of hearing of them from Tongans and Tupaia. See: Thomas, 2004: 332–33.

4   See Teherkézoff, 2008: 15–21

His fleet consisted of his flagship *Arend,* commanded by Jan Koster; the *Thienhoven,* commanded by Cornelis Bouman (Baumann); and the *Afrikaansche Galei,* commanded by Roelof Rosendaal. Also on board the *Arend* was Karl Friedrich Behrens who wrote a romantic account of his travels. Some of Captain Bouman's comments also survive. Along with Roggeveen's diaries and biography, published in 1838, they are the only written accounts of Europeans' first contact with Sāmoans.

Roggeveen made landfalls on Chile, Juan Fernández Islands (the location for the fictional *Robinson Crusoe,*) Rapa Nui, which he named Easter Island, and charted the Tuamotu Group before sighting the uninhabited Rose Island of the Sāmoa Group on 13 June 1722. The crew landed and harvested fresh greens for scurvy-suffering sailors. Two days later they sighted the Manu'a Group of Ta'ū, Ofu and Olosega.

A boat, manned by the Mate of the *Thienhoven* and some sailors, was rowed towards the shore where they encountered people in canoes. Amongst the people was a man referred to as 'the lord of the land' or the 'king' accompanied by a fair-skinned young woman wearing a necklace of 'blue beads'. The man gestured towards the beads, inquiring through signs if the Mate had some beads. The Mate nodded and pointed towards the *Thienhoven* where the Sāmoans offered gifts of food: fish, fruit and coconuts. The trade-minded Europeans gave them trinkets in exchange.[5] But the Sāmoans would not leave their canoes to board the ship, and the Dutch never went ashore.

No anchorage was found and the Dutch moved on. Tutuila and 'Upolu were sighted over the next two days. Roggeveen was reluctant to spend time searching for a safe anchorage and, taking advantage of the southeast trade winds, he sailed on towards Batavia leaving the exploration of Sāmoa to others.

Thus ended the first, brief encounter between Sāmoans and Europeans.

The second visitor, French explorer Louis-Antoine de Bougainville,

5   Kramer, 1994, Vol. II: 3–4; Teherkézoff, 2008: 17.

made contact with canoes far out at sea off the coast of Manuʻa on 3 and 4 May 1768. The canoes circled the ships exchanging fruit and shells for trinkets. Bougainville remarked on the 'blue silk cloths' worn by the men, mistaking *peʻa*, tattoos, for trousers. Seeing so many canoes far from shore he gave the islands the name of the 'Isles of the Navigators'. On 5 May Bougainville sailed past Tutuila and headed south. He never landed in Sāmoa. In March 1769 Bougainville completed the first French circumnavigation of the globe, giving his name to a large island in the east of Papua New Guinea, and a beautiful flowering climbing shrub, Bougainvillea.

La Pérouse, who had been on Bougainville's expedition as a junior officer, set out from France in August 1785 with the intention of the 'discovery of new lands and the establishment of trade relationships'. His two ships, *L'Astrolabe* and *Boussole*, sailed around Cape Horn into the Pacific, visiting Chile, Easter Island, Hawaiʻi, California, Manila, the Kamchatka Peninsula, Korea, Japan, Sāmoa, Tonga, and Australia, where he posted home news of his discoveries, before disappearing. The mystery surrounding the fate of the La Pérouse Expedition was finally solved in 1826 when Peter Dillon, an Irish trader, purchased a French sword hilt from a Solomon Islander. Dillon subsequently led an expedition to Vanikoro Island, recovered more relics and stories of the fate of La Pérouse and claimed the 10,000-franc reward that had been offered by the French Government in 1791. The wreckage of the two ships on Vanikoro Reef in the Solomon Islands was conclusively identified by French expeditions in 1990 and 1997.[6]

La Pérouse had sighted Manuʻa on 6 December 1787 and passed between Taʻū and Olosega two days later where boats came out and some coconuts, fruit, birds, a pigeon and a small pig were exchanged for glass beads. The boats dropped anchor at Tutuila on 9 December and 'three armed boats were sent ashore'. The next day trade and exchange continued and a fateful 'misunderstanding' led to the deaths of 12 officers and sailors, and 20 wounded. There is a detailed account about the incident in Kramer,[7] taken from La Pérouse's

6   See Rigby et al., 2018: 128–133, and Gonthier, 1997.
7   Kramer, 1994, Vol. II: 9–14.

account, which portrays the Sāmoans very badly. George Turner later provided a more balanced view of this tragic encounter.[8]

After extracting his expedition from the debacle at Tutuila, La Pérouse sailed on to 'Upolu and Savai'i before he headed to Tonga. La Pérouse's account of the killings led to Sāmoa gaining a reputation for savagery and consequently many future mariners avoided Sāmoa.

One of the few ships that visited Sāmoa in the next two decades was the HMS *Pandora*, commanded by Captain Edward Edwards, searching for the *Bounty* mutineers. They captured 14 mutineers in Tahiti but did not find the rest who were hiding on the uncharted Pitcairn Island. The ship briefly entered Pago Pago Harbour in 1791, had a hostile encounter with the local people and quickly departed. The HMS *Pandora* ran aground on the Great Barrier Reef with loss of some crew and prisoners. The remainder made the voyage to Timor on the ship's boats and eventually 78 of the 134 men on board made it back to England. Three of the prisoners, having survived shipwreck and the voyage home, were executed on 29 October 1792 for their mutiny on the *Bounty*.

At the end of the 18th century Sāmoa remained relatively unexplored and undisturbed by Europeans. In the first three decades of the 19th century few ships visited but a handful of sailors and escaped convicts managed to find refuge in Sāmoa.

George Bass, who supplied provisions to the British penal colony at Botany Bay, visited Tutuila in 1802 looking for supplies of fruit and vegetables. He 'found the Sāmoans he encountered friendly and receptive' and an Englishman, David Sherlock, living there, happily married and with several children. Sherlock declined the offer of a passage home.[9] Whalers and traders visited many Pacific Islands, including Sāmoa, but few kept records of their visits. Theirs is a largely unwritten history.

A Russian, Otto von Kotzebue, was the next European explorer to resume contact. In early April 1824 he sighted Rose Atoll, sailed past Manu'a, and hove to off Tutuila where there was some trading.

8   See Turner, 1884: 196.
9   See Gilson, 1970: 67.

A fracas ensued with Sāmoans who had climbed on to the ship and were subsequently thrown overboard. Kotzebue quickly proceeded to 'Upolu.

At Aleipata he observed fishermen who '. . . handed over their fish and waited calmly to see what we would give them in exchange and were always quite satisfied'. At Manono further trading took place and a large elegant canoe, rowed by ten men, with a chiefly man holding '. . . an opened green silken European umbrella' came up to the ship. He was invited on board and asked for the *'eigeh'* (*ali'i*) and presented three large pigs and fruit to Kotzebue who reciprocated with blue glass beads, other trinkets and an axe. The chief was described as '. . . completely untattooed, about six feet tall and very lean, otherwise of strong muscles and vigorous. His face was not handsome but engaging. He displayed intelligence and circumspectness; his behaviour was modest and proper.' 'His attire consisted of a very finely woven grass mat, which hung like a short coat around his shoulders, and of a belt. His head was wrapped in a piece of white material in the shape of a turban.'[10]

This was the first detailed written description of a chiefly Sāmoan man. Kramer, after reading Kotzebue's account a century later, speculated that this man was the Manono chief Lei'ataua Tonumaipe'a Tamafaigā. Kotzebue's observation of his umbrella, and a Spanish coin in the chief's procession, reinforced the view that Sāmoans were already acquainted with European products, despite none having apparently landed on the western islands. The answer to that mystery is to be found in the presence of adventurers known collectively as 'beachcombers'.

Adventurers–Beachcombers

Following in the wake of the earlier explorers, a 'straggle of bold captains'[11] set out to seek their fortunes in the Pacific. From the late 18th century and into the 19th century they sought whales, *bêche-*

10 See Kramer, 1994, Vol. II: 22
11 See Richards, 2017, *Bold Captains*, Vols 1 & 2.

de-mere, sandalwood and other tradeable commodities including people. Piracy was not unknown and slavery, including the later notorious 'blackbirding' of people for plantation labour, is written in some of the darker chapters of Pacific Island history.[12] From time to time sailors would 'jump ship' to pursue onshore their fortune, adventure, or women. Others were shipwrecked or marooned. A few, like Herman Melville[13] and William Mariner,[14] lived to tell the tale.

A ragtag population of beachcombers, escaped convicts and various adventurers, living outside of the law, were randomly scattered across the Pacific.[15] Early beachcombers, adventurers and other castaways were usually temporary residents who became integrated into the indigenous communities upon whom they were dependent for their livelihood. They had skills and knowledge that were useful in translating and transacting relationships and trade with visiting ships, and '. . . a spirit of genuine and mutual affection and understanding between the beachcomber . . . and the people with whom they lived . . .' developed.[16] Later beachcombers were more likely escaped convicts from the penal settlements in Australia. Some washed up in Sāmoa, including Irish Tom, an escaped convict who lived on Manono under the protection of the chief Tamafaigā. When John Williams arrived in 1830 he noted '. . . there were apparently twenty-five whites in the group [Sāmoa]; the most unruly convicts had by then been killed and there was a leavening of better educated people among them, such as Stevens, the surgeon of the whaler *Oldham*.'

The 'beachcomber era' spanned the time between European explorers and missionaries and settlers. The beachcombers left

12 See Maude, 1981, *Slavers in Paradise*.
13 Herman Melville was first to use the term 'beachcomber' and wrote *Typee – A Peep at Polynesian Life*, 1846, and *Omoo – A Narrative of Adventures in the South Seas*, 1847, romantic stories based loosely on his time as a beachcomber in Tahiti in the early 1840s.
14 See Martin, 1991 (first published in 1817), *Tonga Islands – William Mariner's Account . . . of his four years in Tonga after surviving a massacre and being adopted by Finau 'Ulukalala*.
15 See Maude, 1968: 134–177, *Of Islands and Men*, Chapter 4: 'Beachcombers and Castaways'; and Campbell, 1991: 66–67.
16 Maude, 1968: 168.

two legacies: their DNA and their stories. The latter provide some insights into Sāmoan life and customs before the impact of European settlement; the former can be found in their descendants' complexions and character.

Missionaries

'First the missionary, then the Consul and at last the invading army.' J.A. Hobson, the British historian, succinctly summarised imperial expansion.[17] Local people, the 'beneficiaries' of missionary activity, would later sadly say: 'First they had the Bible and we had the land; now we have the Bible and they have the land.' Both of these, often quoted, sayings simplify the complex, mixed and long-lasting legacy of missionaries in Sāmoa. Literacy, the many other skills gained in the education programmes of religious schools, and the education and expansion of opportunities for women are amongst the many positive outcomes of the 19th century missionaries' work in Sāmoa.

Missionary activity, the expansion of trade and state formation started in Polynesia in the early 1800s. Alongside commerce and conversion to the Christian God, the missionaries introduced a 'code of Christian Laws'. In Tahiti a unified kingdom was established under the rule of the Pomare dynasty and a parliament established in 1824. Earlier, Hawai'i was unified under Kamehameha I. Traders and missionaries benefited when island groups were politically unified and peaceful. Commerce and conversion went hand in hand; state formation soon followed.

Sāmoans were '. . . a polytheistic and practical people, tolerant to the gods of other men and inclined to judge a deity on the favours he lavished on the living'. Prior to 1830 a few Sāmoans had come into contact with the Christian faith in Tonga and Tahiti and had returned home as nominal Christians. Siovili (Joe Gimlet) established a Christian-inspired millenarian cult on Savai'i and 'Upolu, and a number of 'sailor sects' were founded by castaways living in Sāmoan

17 Hobson, 1938: 204.

villages.[18] These home-grown, informal *lotu* soon faded under the stern gaze of missionaries from the mainstream churches.[19]

The arrival of Christian missionaries had an impact that is echoed today in the governance of Sāmoa. *Fa'avae I Le Atua Sāmoa, A nation founded on God*, is the motto inscribed on the Sāmoan Coat of Arms and enshrined in the *Constitution of the Independent State of Sāmoa*.

In 1830 John Williams, of the London Missionary Society (LMS), was the first Christian missionary to arrive in Sāmoa, followed by the Wesleyan Methodist Mission in 1835. The French Roman Catholics arrived in 1845 and the Church of Jesus Christ of Latter-Day Saints, the Mormons, in 1863. These four denominations would dominate religious life in Sāmoa for the next century.

The London Missionary Society

On Sunday 18 July 1830 *The Messenger of Peace* anchored near Sapapāli'i with the Reverend John Williams and six Polynesian mission teachers on board, accompanied by Faueā, a Sāmoan chief Williams had met in Tonga.

Faueā had been away from Sāmoa for a decade and played an important role in negotiating Williams' first encounter with Sāmoa. Faueā directed Williams to Sapapāli'i, in the Fa'asāleleaga district of Savai'i, the home of Malietoa Vai'inupō, chief of Sā Malietoa. In the absence of Malietoa Vai'inupō, they were met by Taimalelagi, a relative of Faueā, and Malietoa Vai'inupō's younger half-brother. Faueā told the people that the ship was a *va'a lotu*, a ship bringing the Christian faith, and would bring peace and abundant goods to those who joined the faith. Faueā's rhetoric and connections eased Williams' entry into Sāmoan society and helped him to establish a

18 See Gilson, 1970: 69–77. Most of these cults and sects were small and localised, and few outlived their founders. Most adherents succumbed to missionary pressure, and the cults and sects were abandoned.

19 Aaron Buzacott, 1866: 127 tells the story of the Savai'ian Siovili (Joe Gimlet) and the 'lotus bred of darkness and folly, before the light of the glorious gospel of Jesus Christ'. In 1836 Buzacott also met, and denounced, several runaway sailors who had set up 'sailor religions'.

base for his missionary work.

Malietoa Vaiʻinupō soon returned from Āʻana, where he had been exacting revenge on Fasitoʻotai for their part in the death of the chief of Manono, Leiataua Tonumaipeʻa Tamafaigā. Williams' arrival coincided with a pause in civil warfare.

Malietoa Vaiʻinupō met with Williams who explained his mission and talked about the Christian Gospel. They exchanged gifts. Malietoa agreed to receive Mission teachers, he and Taimalelagi offered protection to the missionaries to conduct their services and Malietoa Vaiʻinupō said he would end the war quickly and promised to avoid fighting in the future. In turn, Williams said that if Malietoa's promises were kept, he would send European missionaries to live in Sāmoa.

A week after he arrived, Williams left Sāmoa, his mission accomplished.

Williams was pragmatic. He accepted the public declarations of Christian belief by Sāmoan chiefs, did not challenge cultural practices, and exploited the healing power of medicine and the 'magic' of mechanical devices to inspire awe. Williams held to the belief that 'legitimate commerce' was a foundation for 'civilisation'. In 1839 his son, John Chauncer Williams, became the first Christian trader in Sāmoa and played an important role in the development of governance in Sāmoa. Williams Senior was also lucky, and his timing was good. Tamafaigā, who in the previous year had gained the *tafaʻifā* by force, was a powerful and fierce warrior whose timely demise allowed Malietoa Vaiʻinupō to fill the power vacuum.

The arrival of the new religion also fulfilled the prophecy of Nafanua, a *Toa Tamaʻitaʻi*, 'Warrior Princess', who had held the *tafaʻifā*. On her death she was elevated to become a goddess of the pre-Christian Sāmoan religion. Malietoa Fitisemanu, Malietoa Vaiʻinupō's father, sought out Nafanua in a bid to unite Sāmoa, end years of civil war and secure the *tafaʻifā* for his family. Nafanua said: *'Faʻatali i lagi se ao o lou mālō.'* 'Wait on the heavens for a crown for your kingdom.' The arrival of the *papālagi* missionary, preaching the gospel and heralding the arrival of the 'kingdom of heaven', was seen by many as the fulfilment of Nafanua's prophecy, and the new religion was quickly adopted by many Sāmoans for political as well as religious reasons.

The timing of the arrival of Williams cast Malietoa in the role of peacemaker, and the death of Tamafaigā allowed Malietoa Vaiʻinupō to claim the *tafaʻifā*. When he died in 1842 a temporary peace ended and the struggle for the four paramount titles began again.

The London Missionary Society was a nondenominational Protestant church made up of Congregationalists and Free Presbyterians, nonconformists who were opposed to the establishment, episcopacy (the governance of the church by Bishops), and hereditary political power. They preferred a considerable degree of democracy in church and secular life. These principles did not sit well with the hierarchical nature of the *faʻasāmoa*, but the LMS missionaries were pragmatic and needed the patronage and protection of chiefs to pursue their work. The establishment of a theological college at Mālua in 1845 was important because it provided general education as well as theological training for a select group of young men, and their *faletua* wives, who later had important roles to play in the development of Sāmoan society. In time, the *faʻasāmoa* reshaped the LMS into its own image. The LMS rebranded as the Congregational Christian Church of Sāmoa, after independence in 1962, and is now Sāmoa's largest church. The LMS has had a lasting influence on the governance of Sāmoa.

Wesleyan-Methodist Church

In 1822 the first Wesleyan missionary, Walter Lawry, arrived in Tonga. In 1835 Peter Turner and some teachers of the Tongan mission transferred to Sāmoa where they found that Saivaʻaia, a Sāmoan chief who had embraced Christianity during a visit to Tonga, had been teaching a few basic Christian principles in Sāmoa since 1828 and had 2,000 adherents who followed his *Lotu Toga*.

A competition for converts with the LMS quickly developed into a bitter rivalry creating splits between villages. An agreement was reached with the LMS headquarters in London and the Wesleyan mission was disbanded in 1839. However, some of the Wesleyans maintained their separate churches, with help from Tongan teachers. This situation did not last for long. In 1855 the Australian Conference of the Methodist Church took over the South Seas Missions and joined the Wesleyans in Tonga, re-establishing a Wesleyan Methodist mission in Sāmoa in 1857.

The Sāmoan Methodist Church became an independent Conference in 1964 following Sāmoa's independence. Today the Church has a congregation of around 40,000 supporting a theological college, many village churches, and preschools, primary and secondary schools throughout Sāmoa.

Roman Catholic Church

British Protestant missionaries led the establishment of Christian churches in Sāmoa. LMS and Wesleyan missionaries, though in competition with each other, were united in working to contain Roman Catholicism, linking it with French colonial ambitions in Polynesia. Anti-Catholic sermons were preached from Protestant pulpits but did not deter the Roman Catholics.

The first Marist missionaries, Father Roudaire and Father Violette, arrived in Sāmoa from Wallis Island in September 1845 on *l'Étoile de la Mer*. Their first success was in Savai'i where Tuala, chief of Lealatele, converted to *Lotu Pope*. Next they called into Apia Bay where Protestant missionaries were anti-Catholic and anti-French. Due to a stroke of luck they recruited a chief of high rank, Matā'afa Tafagamanu, a contender for the Tui Ātua title, to act as their patron.

Ten years earlier, Matā'afa and his crew had been caught in a storm when sailing between 'Upolu and Tutuila and blown off course, ended up drifting to Wallis Island. Here they were rescued and given hospitality by the pagan chief Lavelua who helped them to return to Sāmoa. Lavelua was subsequently converted to Catholicism by Marist priests. When the Marist missionaries left Wallis for Sāmoa Lavelua asked them to seek out Matā'afa with a request to secure a place for the Catholic mission in Sāmoa. Matā'afa came to Mulinu'u to hear the Marists tell of Lavelua's request, and was honour-bound to protect the priests and thus fulfil his longstanding obligation for

Lavelua's life-saving hospitality. He asked the high chief Faumuinā and others to do the same. Through this remarkable coincidence, the Marists gained protection and a foothold near Apia, gradually gaining a following from former adherents to the declining Siovili cult and lapsed Wesleyans.

Father Roudaire's safety and religious freedom was guaranteed by the chiefs, who also gave him the use of a Sāmoan house at Mulinu'u. French interests were further advanced in Apia by the *Société Français de l'Océanie* (SFO), dedicated to establishing mission stations and trade stores throughout the Pacific Islands. A trading store was established at Mulinu'u, on land given to the Marists, and a SFO merchant, M. Chauvel, started trading in 1847. A year later the store was destroyed by fire, rebuilt, then destroyed by a cyclone. In 1852 the luckless SFO was dissolved and French trade in Sāmoa ended. But the Marist priests were steadfast; they had come to stay and slowly grew their church community.

The Marists tolerated tattooing and other cultural practices that the Protestants had condemned, which made their faith attractive to Sāmoans, and the anti-French political stigma gradually faded. The conversion of Matā'afa Tafagamanu from Methodism to Roman Catholicism further strengthened the Marist's position and status in Sāmoa. Today the Roman Catholic Church is Sāmoa's second largest Christian denomination and worships in a new basilica at Mulivai.

Church of the Latter Day Saints

In 1863 Kimo Pelia and Samuela Manoa, two Hawaiian Mormon missionaries, were sent to Sāmoa by Walter Murray Gibson, who was later excommunicated from the LDS for taking the grand title 'President of the Islands of the Sea and of the Hawaiian Islands for the Church of Jesus Christ of Latter-Day Saints' and engaging in a heresy. For over twenty years Pelia and Manoa laboured and made few conversions. When Pelia died the church also faded out. In 1888, in a belated response to a letter from Manoa seeking official missionaries, Joseph Dean and Harry Moors were sent to Sāmoa. Their mission thrived. By 1891 the LDS mission was headquartered in Apia with small congregations established throughout Sāmoa.

In the early years there were clashes with the mainstream churches, some villages banned the LDS and *matai* publicly condemned the Mormons' aggressive conversion tactics. The Church refrained from political and cultural matters and largely focused on their congregations, their theology and their mission. Over time, the LDS has gained acceptance in Sāmoa. Today, the Church of the Latter Day Saints has a Sāmoan membership of over 33,000.

Establishing Governance

When Europeans arrived in Sāmoa they recognised there were village governments operating and some villages working together at a district level, but they could not identify any central or national government. The basic requirements for governance of a nation state are the establishment of a state and state institutions, the rule of law and mechanisms of accountability. Early attempts were made by Europeans to regulate trade, control the behaviour of residents and visitors, and establish some basic laws. These were the first steps towards establishing formal governance in Sāmoa.

Captain Charles Bethune, Master of the HMS *Conway*, came to Sāmoa seeking escaped convicts from the Australian penal colonies. In December 1837, at Pago Pago harbour, he met with the principal chiefs of Tutuila and presented a draft set of Port Regulations to control shipping, establish a levy for pilots and set a port fee. The regulations also banned port work on the Sabbath, prohibited liquor trade, set a curfew for sailors to be on board from 8pm to daylight, controlled foreign immigration, and set rules for the capture of deserters. The Port Regulations were '. . . by order of the government' and enacted by the Tutuila chiefs with Bethune acting on behalf of Britain.

In January 1838 Bethune was at Apia where he invited the chiefs of 'Upolu to meet with him and a Port Code was adopted, based on the Tutuila Port Regulations and including some clauses on their enforcement by the district chiefs. The Port Regulations had a limited impact on Pago Pago and Apia, where village chiefs had some authority, but had little impact beyond the ports. As only Great

Britain had endorsed the codes, American whalers and others were '. . . ill disposed to the observance of the port controls'.[20] The Port Regulations, aimed at regulating the behaviour of Europeans and Sāmoans, were the first attempt at formal governance. However, as there were no officials to monitor and enforce the regulations, they had limited impact until European consuls were appointed.

The Foreign Consuls

From 1839 British, American, and later French and German, consuls were appointed to defend the interests of their nationals settling and trading in Sāmoa. The first consuls were not solely diplomats; they were also merchants and missionaries. Their divided loyalties led to conflicts of interest that reduced their effectiveness.

In the early 1800s Great Britain, France, the United States of America and Germany were starting to take an interest in the Pacific Islands. Britain had a consul in Tahiti, George Pritchard, '. . . whose legal jurisdiction extended, legally, if not very effectively, through Western Polynesia.'[21] Pritchard, a former LMS representative, visited Sāmoa with John Williams in 1839. He appointed W.C. Cunningham as resident vice-consul '. . . devoted at least as much to projects of political reform and to the control of Sāmoa's "worthless whites" as to the development of the group's commercial potentialities for Britain'.

Cunningham was Sāmoa's first resident European official. The Americans arrived later in the year when Lieutenant Charles Wilkes led the United States Exploring Expedition to Sāmoa. Wilkes had a broad brief 'to promote the advancement of civilization and commerce' and investigate the killing of several Americans. He drafted a new Port Code that extended and superseded Bethune's Port Regulations and 'concluded that chiefs must . . . explicitly guarantee foreign residents and visitors certain fundamental rights and agree to protect their lives and property'. Wilkes appointed John C. Williams, the missionary's

20 See Gilson, 1970: 147–150.
21 See Gilson, 1970: 150.

son, as American consular representative. Again, the new Code was unevenly administered and had limited success in keeping order. However, it placed American ships on the same footing as the British.

The Growth of Trade and Settlement

Today, the city of Apia is the largest urban settlement in Sāmoa. In the 1830s the foreshore of the bay was almost deserted; one village, Apia, lay between the Vaisigano River and the Mulivai stream. At that time the Matāutu area to the east was a deserted, sacred, forbidden point of land, and Mulinu'u to the west was a thin strip of land bounded by an extensive mangrove swamp, a *taufusi*. Most of the Sāmoans in the district lived inland in Vaimoso, Lepea and Vailoa villages at Faleata, and Moto'otua, Tanugāmanono and Magiagi villages in the

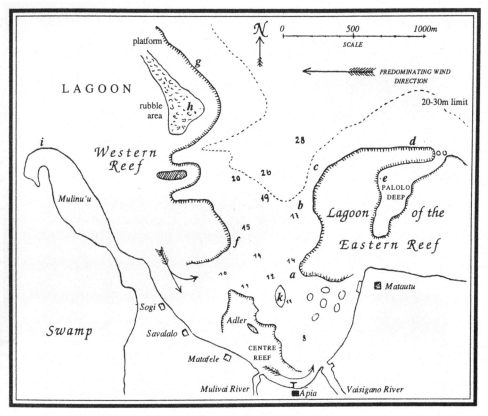

Apia Harbour, 19th Century
(Krämer, *The Samoa Islands* II, Polynesian Press, 1995)

Vaimauga district. Apia Bay attracted European settlement due to its harbour, central location and substantial unoccupied beach land.

Cunningham leased some land at Apia and by 1840 had built a consulate and storehouse for trade. He did not prosper and left Sāmoa in 1842. J.C. Williams, through his LMS connections, purchased four acres of land at Fagali'i for a house site and agricultural purposes and a section in Apia for his consular and commercial headquarters. Williams' commercial success was based on American whaler traffic, the supply of provisions to mission stations and trade in coconut oil. Other traders soon followed and the Apia settlement expanded.

European settlement attracted Sāmoan attention and settlement around Apia Bay. Seumanutafa Pogai, the senior chief of Apia village, was the first local contact point for foreigners wanting land, food supplies, fresh water and labour. Under the Port Regulations, he also received all the port fees. By 1850 To'omalatai Toetagata, the Vaimauga chief who had lived at Moto'otua, shifted his people to Matāutu, overcoming fear of pagan spirits, to be closer to the commercial activity. Faumuinā and people from Faleata started to settle in Mulinu'u and spread to Savalalo. Matafele was then occupied by people from Tanugāmanono.

George Pritchard, who had been deported from Tahiti by the French for opposing their intervention in local affairs, made an ignominious return to Apia in 1845 to re-establish a British consular presence following Cunningham's departure. A man of influence in Tahiti, Pritchard had been British Consul, merchant, clergyman, magistrate and principal adviser to Pomare's Tahitian government. Pritchard had travelled to England seeking redress but the Foreign Office had abandoned Tahiti to the French, declined a request from Tutuila's chiefs for British Protectorate status for Sāmoa, and sent him to be British Consul in Apia. Though supported by LMS friends, Pritchard was considered *vāivai*, weak, tired, a loser, by Sāmoans, and was unable to secure land. He built a small shack at Savalalo. British influence was in temporary decline, accelerated by the French priests' arrival and M. Chauvel establishing the SFO trading store at Mulinu'u. Late in 1846 the first French ships arrived bringing staff for the mission and goods in trade for coconut oil. The SFO initially prospered and the scene was set for European rivalry.

However, there was a very limited market in Sāmoa. Chauvel cornered the trade in coconut oil, J.C. Williams supplied the Protestant missions with supplies, and Pritchard barely scraped a living. Pritchard sent dispatches to the British Foreign Office alerting them to French 'political intervention'. Chauvel claimed to represent France, but had no formal credentials. At this early stage, 'Great Power Rivalry' was in reality a malicious squabble between local merchants for trade in a tiny marketplace.

The beginning of the end for French trade in Sāmoa was the arson of Chauvel's trade store at Mulinu'u by an unknown European, which strangely was never officially reported by the British or American consuls. Pritchard and Williams apparently 'looked the other way'.

Pritchard's dispatches to the Foreign Office eventually bore fruit and ships from the Royal Navy arrived enhancing his status as British Consul, which allowed him to move from Savalalo and buy land at Mulivai for his consulate and business.

Meanwhile, the Apia chief Seumanutafa Pogai kept control over trade and settlement in Apia Bay, preventing the importation of liquor and barring all but LMS missionaries from settling. Apia was the only safe port for shipping and trade began to flourish as ship visits, to purchase supplies and fresh water, increased due to the discovery of gold in California and Australia. With increased shipping the local liquor laws became increasingly unpopular with sailors and the British and American consuls were under pressure. They were churchmen, consuls and merchants with mixed and competing objectives.

Pritchard was the first to weaken. In 1850 he imported a cargo of spirits for the port trade and put it under his consular protection. In 1852 he imported a second shipment. The former missionary was consequently expelled from the London Missionary Society and Apia was never again a 'dry' port. Compounding this 'betrayal', Pritchard sold his land at Mulivai to the Marists, where they built their first basilica, and he shifted his operations to Matāutu. For this 'sin' he was excommunicated from the LMS.

A civil war,[22] that had broken out in 1848, safety considerations, the location of the port and the increased availability of land for sale led most Europeans to settle around Apia Bay. The business community rapidly expanded and by the mid 1850s most of the foreshore between Sogi and Matāutu had been occupied. In 1856, 75 foreigners lived more or less permanently in Apia, by 1860 the 100 residents were often outnumbered by visitors and castaways.

British and American traders: J.C. Williams, George Pritchard, W.C. Turnbull, the Hort Brothers, John Sargent, and Aaron Van Camp were among the first to set up businesses. In 1857 the Sāmoan branch of a German company, Johann Cesar Godeffroy und Sohn, from Hamburg, arrived to develop and exploit the growing trade in coconut oil throughout the Pacific.

Apia Bay had begun as a pious, orderly, church-centred community. By the 1850s, lacking formal governance, the 'Beach' was described as a 'hell of the Pacific' and Pritchard's consulate had turned into 'a pot-house'. Grog shops, boarding houses, billiards parlours, blacksmiths, coopers, mechanics, auctioneers and two surgeons had set up for business in Apia, along with the traders' stores.

Village governance throughout Sāmoa continued uninterrupted. *Matai*, through their village *fono*, had local authority and still governed their communities. When Sāmoans offended against Europeans the consuls looked to the village *fono* to take action. The chiefs of Apia had some control of the Europeans on the Beach through the Port Regulations, but Europeans were reluctant to submit to the rule of 'natives' and envisaged some form of government of 'Europeans by Europeans'.

No treaty had been negotiated or signed by Sāmoans; sovereignty had not been ceded, but Sāmoa was not recognised as a sovereign nation. The British and American consuls were limited to acting as magistrates, with jurisdiction over their own citizens, and they were often compromised by their involvement in commercial activities. However, the consuls found support from offshore.

---

22 See more on the civil war, page 54–58 below.

Naval Justice?

British and American warships visited Sāmoa from the 1840s on regular patrols to show the flag and they intervened to maintain peace and establish order. Over time the consuls employed naval justice, or gunboat diplomacy, to settle disputes between Europeans and Sāmoans, and amongst Sāmoans.

So called naval justice was irregular and erratic, as it required a ship to be in Sāmoa and a captain who was motivated to intervene. Wilkes, Commander of the United States Exploring Expedition to Sāmoa, was the first to assert naval justice. Later his second in command, Captain Hudson, attempted to capture Popotunu, a young Sāmoan who was accused of killing an American sailor. Hudson took a number of prominent chiefs hostage, including Malietoa Mōlī, in an attempt to secure the surrender of Popotunu. This failed. In another incident he bombarded and burned three villages at Saluafata Bay, where the local chiefs had refused to surrender another accused murderer.

The Americans intervened in a further incident in 1851 when an American sailor was killed in Apia in a drunken brawl with Portuguese and Tongan seamen. The Portuguese was quickly apprehended but the Tongan ran away to Savai'i. Soon after, the USS *St Mary's*, commanded by Captain Magruder, arrived in Apia. Magruder held Seumanutafa Pogai, the high chief of Apia and signatory to the Port Code, responsible and took him hostage, along with Malietoa Mōlī and a Tongan teacher, demanding that the Tongan sailor was returned from Savai'i. Pogai said that he had no power in Savai'i. A party from Vaimauga was dispatched to Savai'i to fetch the sailor but returned empty-handed. The hostages were released. Captain Magruder then demanded that the chiefs sign a new agreement which required them to deliver up anyone accused of murdering an American, with the threat that their villages would be destroyed and their chiefs 'carried away as captives' if they did not comply. In 1852 the British made a similar declaration.

Hostage taking and threats of naval bombardment were strategies employed by both the Americans and British to exercise justice and settle disputes between Europeans and Sāmoans. The consuls also attempted to mediate between villages to stop civil warfare.

When William Fox was shot dead in his store at Sala'ilua, Savai'i, in 1856, a heated conflict arose between Sala'ilua and Sagone, rival *pule* centres of Itū-o-Fafine. Sailusi, the killer, was a young man of chiefly status from Sagone. The conflict quickly escalated and men from Sala'ilua took vengeance, killing a Sagone chief. The British and American consuls arrived to investigate and attempted to mediate a resolution but had no power to back up their threats so they called on the Navy. Naval justice was brutal but not always swift. It took two years for British warship HMS *Cordelia* to arrive. Sagone was then bombarded, heavy fines were imposed on senior *matai* for delaying the surrender of Sailusi, who was eventually taken on board and tried before a naval court and sentenced to death. To avoid further enflaming the conflict between Sala'ilua and Sagone, the sentence was carried out in Apia.

When war was threatened by Malietoa Taimalelagi against Ā'ana in 1848, European residents called on Captain Worth of HMS *Calypso* to intervene and protect the community. Worth announced that foreign residents, as neutrals, should be free from injury and insult during any conflict between Sāmoans, and that their houses should be marked by flags to indicate their neutrality. He could not stay indefinitely in Sāmoa so when he departed he said that he would soon return and would hold accountable any party who broke these arrangements.

A few days after the *Calypso* left, war broke out and some European houses and property, and the LMS chapel at Leulumoega, were destroyed. On his return, Worth and the consuls Pritchard and Williams agreed, without a trial, that Malietoa Taimalelagi and all the people at Mulinu'u were guilty of breaching the neutrality agreement and should be taught a lesson. Thirteen foreigners claimed a total of US$1,625 in losses, including $1,000 for the destruction of the chapel. Taimalelagi was fined the full amount and ordered to evacuate his forces from Mulinu'u and return home as soon as the fine was paid. The *Calypso* blockaded Mulinu'u, threatening a bombardment and the destruction of canoes and the camp if the fine was not paid in goods and cash within three days. Worth's ultimatum was accepted and, while civil warfare was not ended, an uneasy truce was established through 'naval justice' and the property of Europeans was respected during later conflicts.

Steps Towards Governance

Naval interventions aimed at resolving disputes between Sāmoans and Europeans exposed the need for a more permanent form of governance and led to the formation of the Foreign Residents Society in 1851.

The Foreign Residents Society was 'basically a government of the town-meeting type' open to all settlers with jurisdiction over all Europeans. The leaders were George Pritchard[23] and William Yandall, an English boat builder. The chief purpose of the Society, comprised of a president and judges, was keeping order and settling disputes amongst Europeans on the Beach, including settling minor cases of theft, assault, property damage and indebtedness. The Society had no formal power but fined offenders.[24] This worked reasonably well for minor matters but when major crimes were perpetrated, such as the Van Camp Affair,[25] the weakness of the jurisdiction and the limited powers of the consuls were exposed.

Separating governance of the Europeans by the Europeans from governance of the Sāmoans by the Sāmoans became increasingly difficult.

In 1855 the chiefs of Apia Bay banned Sāmoans from the trade

23 By 1851 George Pritchard had become the sole consul in 'office' in Apia. The Catholic mission asked him to act as French consular agent, and, when J.C. Williams departed, Pritchard managed to acquire the role of 'acting' American commercial agent, all without consultation with the British Government. Far from the capitals of Europe, Pritchard had become the 'people's choice' for the 'triple crown'.

24 See Gilson, 1970: 230–233.

25 Aaron Van Camp was an American adventurer and con-artist who deceived many local businessmen, embezzled funds and was briefly American Consul before decamping. See Gilson, 1970: 230–233.

stores. This boycott can be seen as an assertion of sovereign rule. Seumanutafa Pogai and the other Apia chiefs were unhappy with the high prices of goods, the encroachment of Europeans on their lands and the high-handedness of the consuls in settling disputes. They asked for a price-control law. When this request was refused a boycott was put in place and Sāmoan constables were posted at the stores to enforce it. Naval justice was used to break the boycott.

Captain Fremantle, commander of the HMS *Juno* on a regular visit to Apia, discovered that the tension between the Sāmoans and the Europeans was escalating and called a meeting of the chiefs and traders. The Sāmoans were told that buying and selling was a private matter and that governments do not normally interfere in the marketplace. A compromise was reached whereby the chiefs could continue to control their own people but Sāmoans from elsewhere were free to trade and the constables were removed. The traders accepted the compromise and the boycott soon collapsed.

On a return visit to Apia a year later, Freemantle saw a great improvement in the relationship between Sāmoans and Europeans. He arranged a meeting of the Apia chiefs, Seumanutafa Pogai and Toetagata, and the British and American consuls, Pritchard and Jonathan Jenkins, a retired judge, to review the Port Code and improve infrastructure. The outcome was an agreement to build and maintain a bridge over the Vaisigano River to provide better access to the port. They also agreed to establish a Mixed Court to decide cases between Europeans and Sāmoans and to lessen the dependence on naval justice.

The Mixed Court was established in 1857. It was of a quasi-constitutional nature that combined the authority of the chiefs and the legality of the consuls with jurisdiction limited to the area of Apia Bay where Pogai and Toetagata had traditional authority. The two chiefs and the consuls acted as judges with each to enforce judgements on their own people. The Mixed Court was slow and worked imperfectly but was an important step to improve the administration of justice at a time of transition.

During the second half of the 19th century a number of attempts were made to bring Sāmoans and Europeans together to establish a national government for Sāmoa. J.C. Williams, the British consul, was the leading figure working to establish governance. In 1859 he developed a basic code to protect property and business and took it to the chiefs of the Vaimauga sub-district, which included Apia Bay and the European settlement. In 1860 the chiefs adopted Williams' draft law and appointed executive and judicial officers to implement it.[26] However, chiefs of the wider district of Tuamāsaga objected as they felt that the Vaimauga had wider ambitions, but Williams warned other Sāmoans not to intervene. A Sāmoan police force and prison was established to control public order and the excesses of the beachcombers and 'riff-raff' of the Beach. While the code initially found favour and protected the law-abiding citizens, there were problems. Some of the police became over-zealous and the collection of fines became a convenient source of income for the judges. Goodwill started to fade and a confrontation with August Unshelm, the Godeffroy company manager, tested the limits of action that Sāmoan police could take in relation to Europeans.

When some policemen forced entry to the Godeffroy business at Matafele in pursuit of a Sāmoan woman, Unshelm reacted strongly, threatening to 'crush the Sāmoans' and to bring in a French warship to back up his threat. This came to nothing, as, unfortunately for Unshelm, he was soon after lost at sea in a hurricane.[27]

In December 1865, J.C. Williams again called the principal chiefs and *tulāfale* from all the districts to a meeting in Apia because 'the present state of Sāmoa without either a responsible Government or laws' was a problem. European consuls attempted to mediate national reform and establish a central government. They argued that the Hawai'ians, Tongans, Rarotongans and Niueans were already moving towards governing themselves but the Sāmoans, with their many independent districts, were falling behind and must create a strong central government to gain recognition from foreign powers. Following the example of the Vaimauga, other districts began to establish district codes. Proposals to bring various district codes

---

26 Other districts, Ā'ana and north-western Tuamāsaga, adopted similar codes.
27 See Gilson, 1970: 250–252.

together ran up against the pride, ambitions and the rivalries of the *fa'asāmoa*. Districts and villages would not obey the decisions of a government where they were not directly represented, and the ongoing dispute over the Malietoa title complicated the political situation amongst Sāmoans.

Attempts to establish a joint government collapsed when Europeans would not accept the authority of the Sāmoan chiefs. Subsequently the Foreign Residents Society was reformed becoming the Association for the Mutual Protection of Life and Property. Williams was elected as Judge with jurisdiction over all Europeans. However, Williams' appointment was not accepted by the Americans or the British Foreign Office so he resigned but continued to act as a magistrate. Meantime, Theodore Weber had succeeded Unshelm at Godeffroy and Son as the Hamburg consul and Jonas Coe was commissioned as the United States commercial agent and consul. These two worked well, together with Williams, in the Association, managing settlers' interests until the 1870s.

Civil War

During the 19th century, as Sāmoa was taking slow steps towards the establishment of governance, there was a series of civil wars between rival Sāmoan factions. These wars were in the main part contests for paramount titles. Meleisea[28] provides a succinct overview of the major alliances:

> There were two major political divisions in the 1830s. One was Tuamāsaga district on the island of 'Upolu, allied with a number of districts on the island of Savai'i and the small islands of Apolima and Manono (known as "Aiga i le Tai" – the family of the sea). The other was the district of Ā'ana and Ātua on the island of 'Upolu. The Sa Tupua and the orator groups of Tumua were dominant in Ā'ana and Ātua, whereas the other district[s] were allied with Malietoa and the orator groups of Pule. The Sa Malietoa had

28 Meleisea, 1987: 22.

headquarters in both Tuamāsaga, at Malie, and in the Savai'i district of Fa'asaleleaga, at Sapapāli'i.

The balance of power between the competing factions shifted back and forth during the civil wars; the victors were referred to as the *mālō* and the vanquished as *vāivai*.[29]

When Malietoa Vai'inupō died in 1841, his half-brother Taimalelagi succeeded him for the Malietoa title, and the other three paramount titles of the *tafa'ifā* were dispersed and contested.[30] An inconclusive six-year civil war ran from 1848 with succession to the Malietoa title as the main motivation. There was a brief peace when Mōlī (Vai'inupō's eldest son) was appointed Malietoa, but he died in 1858 and the battle resumed. Two rival claimants, Laupepa (Mōlī's son) and Talavou (Vai'inupō's younger son, half-brother of Mōlī), contested the paramount title. The young Laupepa would ordinarily have been expected to wait and succeed Talavou, but Talavou was said to have a 'heathenish hatred' of the LMS and favoured warfare in contrast to the 'peace-loving' Laupepa who had been a student at the Mālua seminary and a LMS teacher. The Europeans favoured Laupepa, who had the support of Tuamāsaga and most of 'Upolu, whereas Talavou had the support of Savai'i and Manono. As one could not gain the advantage over the other, each was installed as a 'Malietoa' by their rival groups of supporters. The rivalry was exacerbated when the European consuls urged the establishment of a representative council, the formation of a centre of government at Matāutu Village, and the choosing of a head of state at a Tuamāsaga district meeting in early 1868.

Supporters used this opportunity to claim that Laupepa was the sole Malietoa, 'King' of Tuamāsaga, and they brought him from Malie to live at Matāutu. The supporters of Talavou quickly set up a rival 'Malietoa government' at Mulinu'u aided by the Faleata chiefs and

29 See Meleisea, 1995: 27.
30 Malietoa Vai'inupō was the last to hold the *tafa'ifā*, and willed that the title would die with him. However, the contest for paramount titles remains alive today. Matā'afa Fagamanu became the Tui Ātua, Tuimaleali'ifano Sualauvi, a close relative of Malietoa Vai'inupō, became the Tui Ā'ana.

backed up by people from Savai'i and Manono. 'For several months thereafter the two factions glared at one another across Apia Bay, both threatening war but neither taking an irrevocable step towards it, until the *faitasiga,* confederation or union of the districts, became the subject of partisan negotiations.'[31]

Some chiefs from Ātua and Ā'ana came to Apia to mediate the Malietoa dispute and promote a union of districts. Talavou supporters participated in the *Faitasiga* movement, as a means of promoting his cause. These 'Unionists' gained local European support for a united government to end the dispute peacefully and appeared to have the stronger force if war eventuated. However, mediation was unsuccessful as the rivalries ran very deep, allegiances were volatile and European involvement was often naïve, self-serving, uninformed or misguided.

The rivalry between Laupepa and Talavou was one factor that contributed to the *Faitasiga* (unification) wars from 1869 to 1873.[32] Another factor was that European settlers had now acquired a large economic stake in Sāmoa through the development of plantations and the importation of indentured labour to clear land, and cultivate and process copra and cotton. Acquiring land and protecting their investment in land and infrastructure was the prime European motivation for improving governance, and installing a unified national government the aim.

The consuls attempted to establish a neutral zone in Apia Bay to provide protection for European settlers whose property was identified by British and other flags. Armed Sāmoans were banned from the zone. Whilst J.C. Williams claimed he was neutral in the conflict, critics said that he was not impartial because he had promoted the reform movement at Tuamāsaga to members of the LMS; his consulate and business was based at Matautu, and he publicly supported the Laupepa-led Malietoa 'government'. Talavou had identified himself with the Catholics and the rivalry took on a sectarian flavour.

A bloody civil war broke out. Laupepa's armed warriors had refused to leave their Matautu stronghold and set up a barricade near

31 Gilson, 1970: 262.
32 Robert Louis Stevenson provides a lively account of the civil war in *A Footnote to History – Eight Years of Trouble in Sāmoa*, published in 1892.

Mulivai, violating the neutral zone. The Unionist forces from Savai'i, Manono, Ātua and Ā'ana stormed the barricades, took control of the Apia area and destroyed villages in northern Tuamāsaga, driving their opponents into the bush. Some of Williams' family property was destroyed or stolen and a British flag was torn down and destroyed.

In earlier times warfare had been limited to the use of local weapons, materials and supplies, but the availability of guns, sold by unscrupulous traders, changed the balance of power. Commodities such as coconut oil and cotton crops were bartered to purchase weapons. However, when commodities ran short, due to scarcity and drought, land was sold to Europeans for cash to buy guns. Prior to 1870 only small parcels of land had been sold and there was a strong resistance amongst Sāmoans to selling land to Europeans for settlement or the development of large plantations. From 1870, Sāmoans, distracted by the contest for the paramount titles, started to sell large areas of land resulting in the promised sale of two and a half times the total land area of Sāmoa. Many of the land sales were suspect and were later subject to legal land claims. Settlers now had a very strong interest in establishing a government that could uphold their land claims through formally registering land sales and guaranteeing title.

Theodore Weber, the Godeffroy & Son manager, led the rush on Sāmoan land. Between 1869 and 1872 he purchased more than 25,000 acres, most close to Apia. Sāmoan land is communal and local chiefs are their communities' guardians, and stewards of the land associated with their titles. There were situations where land was sold by chiefs who were not resident, but claimed 'ownership' through *gafa* connections. In other cases residents were absent because of the war, or other reasons, and returned to find their land sold. In one well-documented, notorious case, 500 acres of prime land at Vaitele in the pro-Laupepa village of Faleata was sold to Weber by two outsiders who claimed ownership. Tamasese Titimaea, a war leader of the Unionist side, and Faumuinā, received 51 guns in exchange for the land. Other chiefs, who shared the guns, signed the land deed as witnesses. Tamasese Titimaea had never lived at Vaitele but used his ties with the Matai'a family of Faleata and the most important

ali'i of the village, Galumalemana, to convince Weber of his right
to sell the land. In the Sāmoan world no *matai* had sole rights of
land ownership, but Weber and others did deals with individuals and
their land deeds were recognised by the Mixed Court. In a footnote
to this deal, Tamasese Titimaea was much later confronted by the
angry, landless people of Vaitele and assaulted after a Mixed Court
hearing into the matter in 1883, 'because he stole our land'. Tamasese
attempted to reverse the deal, but Weber held onto the land, which
became the Vaitele Plantation.[33]

Another major land purchaser in the 1870s was the Central
Polynesian Land and Commercial Company (CPLCC) whose agents
gained interest in 300,000 acres of Sāmoan land, almost half of
the total landmass, through land speculation by 'on deposit' sales.
Most of these sales had limited paperwork, as there was no lawyer in
Sāmoa, they lacked surveys, and there was no compulsory registration
of deeds. Cheating and disputes were rife. Attempts were made
to regulate land sales but they failed because there was no formal
government to enforce the regulations.

By 1873 the Faitasiga War had fizzled out. The opposing sides
had fought to a standstill, naval interventions had distracted the
belligerents, resources were depleted as the sale of land for weapons
had dried up. As most Sāmoans had taken sides in the conflict, there
was no eminent, neutral person who could mediate a face-saving
settlement. Consequently, the missions and consuls stepped in and
on 1 May 1873 the leaders of the two sides agreed to declare the war
was at an end and to send their warriors home.

Attempts to form a Government

From 1873 to 1876 there was a series of short-lived attempts made by
Sāmoan chiefs, foreign consuls and a fraudster, Albert B. Steinberger,
to form a government in Sāmoa, including the installation of Malietoa
Laupepa as 'King' with support from Ta'imua and Faipule.[34] The

33 See Gilson, 1970: 287.
34 Albert B. Steinberger, an acquaintance of US President Grant, developed
   an elaborate scheme for the governance of Sāmoa. Steinberger was an

Americans worked with the chiefs of Tutuila to establish a naval station in Pago Pago, while the British and Germans focused on the larger islands of the west. All attempts at establishing a stable government failed.[35]

Looking back from our vantage point 150 years later, we can see that there was a missed opportunity available at Easter 1869. If the rival Sāmoan parties had united and put the national interest ahead of their personal ambitions for paramount titles, they could have formed a traditional confederation, a *faitasiga*, a union, a 'parliament of chiefs' to rule a united and independent Sāmoa. At that time, none of the great powers had sufficient military strength to take control of a united Sāmoa. However, the opportunity was lost. Later, Germany would take control because German commercial firms sought imperial protection, and trade offs with other Pacific territories could be made with the British, French and Americans. The growth of the plantation economy, fuelled primarily by European demand for coconut oil and copra, required land for plantations that was sold cheaply to enable both sides of the 'civil war' to purchase firearms.

Today, it is easy to identify the injustices of imperialism as a major factor that drove the loss of Sāmoan sovereignty in the 19th century. The situation was more complex. Sāmoan governance was strong at village level, but at the wider district and national levels governance was weak and not unified. Ambition for paramount titles and the *tafa'ifā* were major drivers at district and national levels, over-riding any attempt to develop national unity against the outside forces. Furthermore, petty jealousies, local squabbles between rival factions, and constantly shifting alliances prevented a clear view of the big

unprincipled self-seeking opportunist who was finally exposed as a fraudster, but only after he had established a 'government' with himself as Premier and Chief Judge of the Supreme Court, and roles for the Ta'imua, seven paramount rulers of districts, and Faipule (aka House of Nobles and House of Representatives) and a 'king', with a four-year term alternating between the Malietoa and Tupua families.

35 Gilson devotes a chapter (Chapter, 13, 291–331) to the Steinberger Regime, as an example of a short-lived, ill-fated attempt to bring order to the chaos of 'Western' Sāmoa's governance during the 1870s. Attempts were also made by the United States Navy to annex 'Eastern' Sāmoa to secure a safe harbour.

picture. Disunity, fuelled by personal ambition put ahead of national interests, is a recurring theme throughout the history of Sāmoa's governance and we shall see it has echoes in the 21st century.

Competing European interests within Sāmoa and across the wider Pacific also meant that each of the 'Great Powers' put their own imperial interests ahead of local Sāmoan priorities. The consuls had limited legal power and used their personal influence and the persuasion of naval power to resolve disputes. This makeshift system of justice worked until the 1870s. However, political disorder and civil conflict increased and more formal measures were needed. The United States, Great Britain and Germany provided legal frameworks that applied internationally to formalise the role of their consuls. The American Act of 1860 was applied to Sāmoa when S.S. Foster was appointed US Consul in 1875. The same year, the Western Pacific High Commission was established by Great Britain and Sir Arthur Gordon was appointed High Commissioner, based in Fiji, with a resident deputy commissioner appointed to Sāmoa in 1878. Treaties of friendship and commerce were established with Sāmoa by the US in 1878, and Germany and Great Britain in 1879. These treaties were signed with the Pulefou (new authority) government at Mulinuʻu headed by Talavou.

The Pulefou government had a weak mandate and faced opposition from the previous government in the form of Tupua Tamasese Titimaea, who was the Tui Āʻana, and Matāʻafa Iosefo, the Tui Ātua. Hostilities between the rival factions broke out in October 1876 and threatened the Godeffroy plantations in northern Tuamāsaga and also Mulifanua. The consuls called on the commander of the German warship *Bismarck* to intervene, threats were made and a settlement was negotiated including the establishment of a new government at Mulinuʻu. In this government, Malietoa Talavou was acknowledged as *Tupu* (king), Malietoa Laupepa, *Sui Tupu* (vice-king or premier), and sixteen Taʻimua and thirty-four Faipule were appointed on a district basis.[36] Though the leaders of both sides swore to carry out the agreement, most of those privately opposed the Pulefou government.

36 See Gilson, 1970: 363–4.

There was one exception: Matā'afa Iosefo joined the new regime, taking on the powerful role of *Ta'imua Sili*, chair of the council, leaving Tamasese Titimaea leading the opposing Tupua side. With Talavou aging and ill, and Laupepa's leadership weakened, Matā'afa was in a strong position for future promotion. And, with three of the four *Tama-a-'Aiga* involved, the foreign consuls recognised the new Malietoa government and promised it naval protection.

While the Sāmoans' new government maintained some semblance of sovereignty, they had made major concessions and significant power rested with the Europeans. The consuls' peace settlement had conditions: first, they would approve Malietoa Talavou's successor; and second, the king would have an Executive Council of three Europeans (an American minister of justice, a British minister of public works and a German minister of finance). In other words, most of the important functions of government would be in the hands of Europeans and 'the Sāmoan Government would have the privilege of paying the ministers' salaries'.[37]

Not surprisingly, the Europeans put their own interests first, aiming to improve public works, wharves, roads and bridges, to support the growing plantation economy and raise public funds. A poll tax was enacted but not enforced, as the Sāmoans would only subscribe to fundraising for purposes that they approved, primarily firearms for defence against the rebels who were outside the Malietoa government. Attempts in July 1880 to bring the rebels in Ātua and their allies in Ā'ana into the Malietoa government on board the German warship *Nautilus* broke down. A new war started in Savai'i, soon followed by general hostilities in 'Upolu after the death of Talavou.

Another peace settlement was negotiated on USS *Lakawanna* in July 1881, after protracted negotiations with British, United States and German consuls. Malietoa Laupepa was proclaimed king and Tupua Tamsese Titimaea, the Tui Ā'ana, vice-king in preference to Matā'afa. While a new national government was installed at Mulinu'u, tensions between the Malietoa and Tupua factions continued at the district level, and the Europeans focused on advancing their own commercial

37 Gilson, 1970: 365.

interests. The ongoing instability of government and its limited administrative capacity meant that legal title to land was difficult to secure and claims for payment or compensation unlikely to be settled. This situation did not deter the German firm, Godeffroy and Son, which kept expanding its land holdings and importing hundreds of indentured labourers from Melanesia and China to plant coconuts and grow other crops. These indentured labourers did not come under Sāmoan jurisdiction and acted as a private army that kept Sāmoans off land they felt they owned but had limited legal recourse to claim.

German Expansion

From 1860 to late 1880 Sāmoan-produced crops doubled, and by 1888 Sāmoans were producing more than 3,000 tons of copra annually, about half of the export trade. Godeffroy and Son, reorganised as *Die Deutsche Handels-und Plantagen-Gesellschaft der Südsee Inseln zu Hamburg* (DHPG), was the other major producer of copra. German traders dominated the export business, extending credit to Sāmoans, charging high interest rates and inflated prices for consumer products. As there was no local currency, debased South American dollars were supplied by DHPG, which controlled export pricing.[38] DHPG was expanding its economic stake in the country.

The German consul, Otto Stuebel, and the German navy worked closely with Weber to strengthen German dominance in Sāmoa, upsetting the three-power *Lakawanna* Treaty arrangements and undermining the Laupepa Government. Stuebel got the government to agree that Sāmoans convicted of offences against Germans should be put under German jurisdiction and work off their sentences through forced labour, and Weber gained ownership of the land at Mulinu'u that housed the Laupepa Government. At the same time, the Berlin government was working to undermine British and American claims to Sāmoa as part of the expansion of its sphere of influence in the Pacific. Great Britain's major Pacific imperial interests were in Fiji, Tonga, Micronesia, New Guinea and the Solomon Islands. Germany

38 Gilson, 1970: 378.

also had interests in Micronesia and New Guinea, but Sāmoa was the centre of their ambitions. The United States was coy about having imperial ambitions but was determined on securing the harbour of Pago Pago in Eastern Sāmoa. Washington called for a three-Power inquiry and conference over the future of Sāmoa. While the great powers danced around each other across the Pacific, the local struggle for power in Apia continued.

Germany made three moves to control the governance of Sāmoa. First, Stuebel forced the Laupepa Government off the land at Mulinuʻu, for not paying rent to DHPG, then pushed them out of Apia denying any Sāmoan sovereignty over the municipal area. Malietoa Laupepa retreated to Afega, a Tuamāsaga *pule* centre. Stuebel courted the Tamasese-led camp based at Leulumoega, playing off the rival Sāmoan factions. Second, in January 1887, Weber and Herr Becker, Stuebel's replacement, sent Eugen Brandeis, a DHPG employee and former Bavarian cavalry officer, to Leulumoega to act as 'premier' (*Aliʻi Taʻitaʻi i le Mālō*) of a German-backed, Tamasese-led government.[39] Third, the Germans acknowledged Tupua Tamasese Titimaea as King and assisted him to train an army and buy arms for possible use against Malietoa Laupepa, who was backed by the British.

The German cause was running into opposition from Great Britain and the United States at the long-delayed international conference held in Washington during 1887.[40] A Tamasese–Brandeis *coup d'état* in August 1887 was signalled by a German-led surprise attack that installed Tupua Tamasese in a puppet government at Mulinuʻu with backing from Becker and the naval Commodore Huesner. The senior German naval officer rounded up as many of Sāmoa's high-ranking chiefs as he could find, threatened them into supporting the new regime, and demanded the surrender of Malietoa Laupepa, who was subsequently sent into exile in the German Marshall Islands. A tax

39 Robert Louis Stevenson (1892: 55) wrote of Brandeis: '. . . a romantic and adventurous character. He had courage, integrity, ideas of his own, and loved the employment, the people, and the place. Yet there was a fly in the ointment.' '. . . the immixture of a trading company in political affairs.'
40 Gilson, 1970: 385.

levy was imposed on all Sāmoans and collected by the government that was backed up by five German naval vessels tasked to maintain law and order and collect revenue.

As Premier, Brandeis ran the government's day-to-day administration, exercising personal power to make government appointments, demanding loyalty and administrative efficiency. This suited the German firms and settlers; the non-Germans were in opposition along with most Sāmoans. While Brandeis was an efficient administrator promoting German imperial interests, he misjudged British and American interests and was insensitive to the nuances of Sāmoan traditional leadership. 'The result was that a large majority of Sāmoans, already overburdened by economic exactions and incensed by Tamasese's undeserved position of privilege at Mulinu'u, were whipped into a revolutionary fury that no available force could restrain.'[41]

The tipping point came when Brandeis encouraged Tupua Tamasese Titimaea to take the vacant *Tafa'ifā* titles in a bid to centralise power. In May 1887 Tamasese took the Tui Ātua title for himself and started signing government papers and proclamations as *'Tui Ā'ana Tui Ātua Tamasese, le Tupu o Sāmoa'*. There was a rapid and hostile reaction from the chiefs of Ātua who moved against Tamasese. German naval ships arrested and imprisoned dozens of chiefs in an attempt to settle the situation down. But in September 1888, when further claims were made by Tamasese supporters for him to take up the *pāpā* of Tuamāsaga, and also the Malietoa title, to complete the *Tafa'ifā*, war broke out.

The Tamasese Government warriors were forced out of Mulinu'u by Matā'afa's forces and retreated north to a stockade in the bush. German naval forces intervened as Matā'afa led his warriors against Tamasese, who was supported by German marines, with heavy casualties on both sides.[42] Tensions mounted between the European sides as British and American warships were sent to protect their nationals. Sāmoa was slipping towards an international conflict.

41 Gilson, 1970: 393.
42 Robert Louis Stevenson wrote a vivid account of the war in *A Footnote to History – Eight Years of Trouble in Sāmoa* (1892).

The confrontation between the United States, Imperial Germany and Great Britain from 1887 to 1889 had escalated into a standoff in early 1889 involving three American warships – USS *Vandalia*, USS *Trenton* and USS *Nipsic* – and three German warships – SMS *Adler*, SMS *Olga* and SMS *Eber* – that were keeping each other at bay over several months in Apia harbour. The British warship, HMS *Calliope*, monitored developments.

The standoff ended dramatically on 15 and 16 March 1889 when a massive cyclone wrecked all six warships in the harbour. The *Calliope* was able to escape the harbour and survived the storm. Subsequently, there were protests in Washington, London and Paris from the relatives of the many young sailors and soldiers who had died. Herbert von Bismarck, son of the German Chancellor, invited delegations from the United States and Great Britain to Berlin in April to sort out territorial conflicts in the Pacific. Consequently, the *Treaty of Berlin* was negotiated, concluded and signed on 14 June 1889.[43]

The Treaty of Berlin

The Berlin Conference had allowed Germany to step back and reassess their position. Germany 'swore off active hostilities against the Matāʻafa forces' and blamed Brandeis and the Consul for the war, despite officially sanctioning the coup. Great Britain, the United States and Germany, without any Sāmoan participation, examined options and came up with an agreement, *The Berlin Act*, to form a condominium in which they maintained equal privileges and declared the 'free right of the natives to elect their Chief or King' and recognise 'the independence of the Sāmoan government'. The details of the Act were very complex and cumbersome; however, Europeans maintained all the control. A 'President' and a 'Chief Justice of Sāmoa', both with wide-ranging powers, were to be appointed and paid for by the 'Government of Sāmoa' on binding recommendations from the three powers. The first Chief Justice was Otto Cedercrantz, a Swedish judge, and the first president was Graf Senfft von Pilsach, a German.

43 See Malielegaoi and Swain, 2016: 141–142.

The establishment of the Condominium initially reduced tensions. Positive contributions of the Condominium included: the breaking of the DHPG's monopoly on foreign exchange transactions; the establishment of a banking house in Apia; the settlement of foreign land claims; and the establishment of a land titles registry. However, the Sāmoan economy slowed and plantations stopped enlarging due to international economic factors. Customs duty and taxes barely covered the cost of government administration and there was little infrastructure development, but the administration expanded. There were five different courts.

The Berlin Act allowed the sale and lease of land within Apia, with the written approval of the Chief Justice, but prohibited the sale of land outside of the municipality. Rural land could be leased for up to 40 years with the approval of the Government and the Chief Justice. The Act also established a Land Commission, consisting of 'three impartial persons, one from each power, and a Natives' Advocate', to hear and rule on land claims. A long series of hearings, investigations and rulings by the Commission resolved most of the questionable European land claims, settled many disputes, put much of the land back into the hands of the traditional owners, and gave formal title to land that had been legally acquired.

While the Condominium Government established by the *Berlin Act* led to a period of peace and made progress on land issues, it sidelined Sāmoan participation in governance, passed an unpopular Head Tax, and was wrecked by the question of who would be king of the Sāmoan Government. Tupua Tamasese Titimaea was out of the question, because of his alignment with Germany and subsequent loss of the recent war. Matā'afa Iosefo was also disqualified, because he led the forces that defeated Tamasese and the German marines. That left the exiled Malietoa Laupepa, whom Germany returned to Sāmoa soon after the Berlin Conference, and was then installed by the three powers as king.

As in previous situations when foreign powers had installed a King of Sāmoa, there was limited agreement amongst Sāmoans about the appointment because of the ongoing struggle for paramount titles. In this case, Matā'afa Iosefo and Malietoa Laupepa were contenders for a single Malietoa title. Matā'afa had significant support but was willing to let Malietoa Laupepa rule as king in the meantime. In 1891 Tupua Tamasese Titimaea died, which amplified the struggle for leadership and the now vacant Tui Ā'ana title. Matā'afa maintained his claim on the Malietoa title and moved from Apia to Malie, a strong Malietoa village, setting himself up in opposition to Laupepa's government. The Malietoa people were divided with various alliances supporting each contender. Tensions grew and hostilities broke out, British and American naval commanders harshly intervened against the 'rebels'. In 1893 Matā'afa Iosefo and ten of his prominent chiefs were exiled to the German-ruled Marshall Islands, 24 of the remaining leaders were imprisoned in Sāmoa for three years with hard labour, their lands seized and large fines levied against their villages. This created lasting resentment against Malietoa Laupepa.

British and German warships supported the Laupepa government to collect the unpopular Head Tax, but, after the disastrous cyclone of 1889, they left Sāmoa during each cyclone season, and the government was too weak to govern or enforce tax collection without naval support. Meanwhile, with Matā'afa in exile, new contenders for leadership arose. Tupua Tamasese Lealofi I, the son of Tupua Tamasese Titimaea, gathered support in Ātua and Ā'ana and a new rebellion, centred on Leulumoenga and Lufilufi, gained momentum. Malietoa Laupepa's health began to fail and by the end of 1896 he was an invalid. Who would succeed him?

At 18, Laupepa's son, Tanumafili, was too young in Sāmoan terms to accede to a paramount title and the kingship. So was Fa'alata, the son of Talavou, who also had a claim on the Malietoa title. The strongest contender was Laupepa's old rival, the exiled Matā'afa Iosefo. The dying Malietoa Laupepa was furious, but the chiefs who controlled the Matā'afa title pledged their allegiance to him, and Laupepa finally agreed to ask for Matā'afa's return if the exiled chiefs also took an oath of loyalty to the government. In August 1898 Malietoa Laupepa died, and a month later Matā'afa Iosefo returned to Sāmoa.

Under the *Berlin Act* the king's successor was to be 'duly elected according to the laws and customs of Sāmoa'. Matā'afa Iosefo was not the only contender to succeed Malietoa Laupepa as *Tupu*, King of Sāmoa. Tupua Tamasese Lealofi I and Tanumafili were the other leading candidates. Tūmua and Pule claimed the traditional right to choose the king and on 12 November 1898, at Leulumoega, Matā'afa Iosefo was elected. At a meeting at Mulinu'u three days later, Lauaki Namulau'ulu Mamoe, the prominent leader of Tūmua and Pule, proposed that the consuls be informed that the Sāmoan people wanted Matā'afa Iosefo. Supporters of Tamasese and Tanumafili rejected the right of Tūmua and Pule to choose the king and refused to sign the letter to the consuls declaring Matā'afa king. Tamasese withdrew his bid and proposed that he would be vice-king under Tanumafili. Now there were two clear candidates: Matā'afa and the Tanumafili-Tamasese ticket. The two groups were asked to nominate 13 chiefs each to meet on 27 November with the Chief Justice, William Chambers, who would listen to arguments and determine who was to be Malietoa Laupepa's successor. Lauaki argued for a consensus in support of Matā'afa Iosefo on the basis of the 1881 *Lakawanna Agreement*, which had resolved that Laupepa's successor should come from Sa Tupua. Tanumafili's supporters would not concede and persisted with his candidacy. Both nominations proceeded to a court hearing.

Chambers began the Supreme Court hearings on 19 December 1898. It was claimed that Tanumafili held the Tui Ā'ana, Tui Ātua, Gatoaitele, Tamāsoali'i and Malietoa titles. Lauaki, speaking for Matā'afa Iosefo, disputed this claim, saying that these titles 'had not been conferred accordance with custom' and that at 18 Tanumafili was too young for high office. Lauaki continued to press for a consensus to support Matā'afa. Tanumafili's counsels argued that the protocols of the Berlin Conference ruled Matā'afa Iosefo ineligible to be king. Chambers accepted that argument and on 31 December ruled Malietoa Tanumafili I King of Sāmoa.[44] The reaction was swift.

Many armed Sāmoans had gathered around Apia awaiting the outcome of the Supreme Court case. On 1 January 1899 Matā'afa's supporters advanced on the town and took over Apia. Tanumafili, Tamasese and their chief supporters sought refuge on the HMS

44 Gilson, 1970: 427–428.

Porpoise in the harbour. On 4 January the consuls recognised a provisional government led by Matāʻafa and his chiefs with Dr Raffel, a German, as executive officer.

The provisional government disarmed Tanumafili's warriors and pressured Tanumafili and Tamasese to accept Matāʻafa Iosefo as the only person who could unite Sāmoa. The Germans accepted the provisional government but the British and Americans had reservations and still supported Tanumafili. The American Admiral Kautz arrived in Apia on the USS *Philadelphia* with instructions from his President 'to act in concert with the majority . . . of the Treaty Powers', and promptly declared the provisional government illegal. The Germans responded with their own declaration supporting the provisional government. Civil war resumed.

Matāʻafa's provisional government retreated from Mulinuʻu and set up on the outskirts of Apia where they were shelled by British and American warships. On 23 March Tanumafili was installed as king at Mulinuʻu by his foreign protectors, who supported and armed his government. The rash actions of the British and American consuls and naval forces in Sāmoa came under strong criticism from their own governments. The United States President McKinley apologised to the German Emperor who proposed that the three powers should withdraw their officials and that a tripartite commission should investigate and make recommendations for the future governance of Sāmoa. After some diplomatic manoeuvring, a commission, consisting of senior diplomats Baron Speck von Sternburg, Charles Eliot and Bartlett Tripp, was dispatched and arrived in Apia on 13 May 1899 aboard the USS *Badger*.

An armed truce was already in place and the Commission's first task was to seek a surrender of all arms. This was agreed and the two armies disbanded and returned to their villages. The commissioners agreed that the existence of a kingship was the major problem. Instead of challenging the Chief Justice's decision, they encouraged Tanumafili to step down and continue his education overseas. On 10 June, Tanumafili resigned and the commission abolished the kingship and set to work on recommendations for the future government.

The commission proposed that an Administrator should have

executive power in Sāmoa, a Legislative Council would make the laws, and a Native Assembly of district chiefs would make recommendations to the Administrator and Legislative Council. The commissioners toured the country explaining their proposals and held a meeting of 400 chiefs in Apia, where Tanumafili's and Matāʻafa's parties held an *ifoga*, a traditional reconciliation ceremony, and formally endorsed the proposals. Before the commissioners left Sāmoa and took their proposals back to their political masters, they installed a provisional government composed of the three consuls with Dr Wilhelm Solf, President of the Apia Municipality, as adviser.

The fate of Sāmoa's governance was decided in discussions behind closed doors in the capitals of Europe without Sāmoan participation. The Germans had quickly worked out that the Americans would be happy with Tutuila and Manuʻa under American administration, giving them a coaling port for their navy in the Pacific.[45] The remaining problem was the British, and, with the German Emperor due to visit England in November 1899, there was some urgency to resolve the matter. The outcome was that Germany gave up her treaty rights in Tonga to Great Britain, made some other concessions, shifted boundaries between their spheres of influence in the Solomon Islands, and agreed that all of Sāmoa west of 171° west longitude would belong to Germany. A tripartite agreement was signed on 2 December 1899. At the dawn of the 20th century Germany and the United States of America took over administrative control of a divided Sāmoa.

The Sāmoans were not happy. They were resentful their country had been partitioned. They had lost their independence; their sovereignty had been usurped. Throughout the 19th century Sāmoans had been unable to unify the competing factions and interests within Sāmoa

45 Davies, 2018: 268, notes: 'One of the prominent features of American
    Pacific imperialism is the predilection for islands. Whereas old-fashioned
    imperialists would occupy and directly exploit substantial land areas, the
    Americans have been content to gain control of a chain of relatively small
    insular territories, from which their naval and aerial power can be projected.'
    Eg: the Aleutian Islands, Hawaii, Guam, the Marshall Islands, American
    Sāmoa etc.

and establish an independent, national government of Sāmoans for Sāmoans[46]. Meanwhile foreigners, who had sabotaged Sāmoans' attempts to form a stable government and acquired their land, had taken over the governance of their nation. The anger and grief of these losses would fuel the dream of *Sāmoa mo Sāmoa,* which would take the next six decades to achieve.

46 It is interesting to note the contrasting governance histories of Sāmoa and Tonga. Taufaʻahau Tupou, the contemporary of Malietoa Vaiʻinupō, unified Tonga under a monarchy. See Meleisea, 1987: 42. The recent struggles to establish democratic governance in Tonga are a consequence of a 19th-century decision to centralise rule, establish a kingdom and disestablish chiefly titles. Sāmoa took a different route.

Chapter 3

German Administration 1900–1914

During the fourteen years of German rule, economic and infrastructure development advanced and the plantation economy grew, based on imported Melanesian and Chinese labour. Colonial rule by Germany provided political stability but was paternalistic and undermined Sāmoan political leadership, institutions and participation in governance. The dream of Sāmoan political independence never faded.

German Sāmoa

In February 1900, Germany declared a protectorate over all of Sāmoa, west of 171° longitude west, and on 1 March 1900 the German flag was raised at Mulinuʻu. These actions established Sāmoa as a German territory. No formal treaty was negotiated or signed; sovereignty was not ceded by Sāmoans. However, a hierarchy was established and expressions of loyalty to Kaiser Wilhelm, Emperor of Germany, *Tupu Sili*, highest king, and the new regime were sought from Sāmoan leaders including Matāʻafa Iosefo who was appointed *Aliʻi Sili*, highest chief.

Sāmoa had become a German colony: German Sāmoa.

A recent definition of colonisation clearly describes the situation in Sāmoa from 1900: 'Colonisation is a relationship of domination between an indigenous majority and a minority of foreign invaders. The fundamental decisions affecting the lives of the colonised people are made and implemented by the colonial rulers in pursuit of interests that are defined in a distant metropolis. Rejecting cultural compromises with the colonised population, the colonisers are convinced of their superiority and their ordained mandate to rule.'[1]

Dr Wilhelm Solf was appointed Governor of German Sāmoa. He was a clever and sophisticated man with a degree in law and a doctorate in philosophy, had served the German Foreign Office in Tanganyika and India, and was considered an enlightened administrator. He energetically promoted large-scale plantation agriculture to be the foundation of the country's economic development and promoted the prosperity of the German firm DHPG as the major driver of economic development. The German administration of Sāmoa can be seen as a case study of the relationship between commercial and imperial power. William Dalrymple[2] notes that '. . . commerce and colonisation have so often walked in lockstep. For western imperialism and corporate capitalism were born at the same time . . .'

In the areas of politics and administration, Solf initially retained the structures and laws established by the Sāmoan government at Mulinu'u that he had inherited, and worked with the *Mālō* of Matā'afa and the leaders of Tūmua and Pule. However, changes were soon made. New government departments were established, staffed in the main by German officers. The Apia municipality was abolished and was replaced by a government Council of senior officials and European residents to advise the Governor on matters of policy. Solf also established a 'native' administration, starting with the appointment of a *Fa'amasino Sili* (Sāmoan Chief Judge) subordinate to the Imperial Judge. Positions of *Ta'ita'i Itū*, District Chiefs; *Fa'amasino Itūmālō*, District Judges; *Pulenu'u*, Village Mayors; *Failautusi*, District Clerks, and *Leoleo*, Constables, were also established and appointments made of loyal supporters of the German administration.

Germany had a plan to transform Sāmoa into a modern, bureaucratic state, an imperial territory contributing to the wealth of the Fatherland. A government had been established, the rule of law was in place, and the institutions of the state were being built, closely associated with a major commercial enterprise.

Road building and other public works were undertaken, funded

1   Osterhammel, 2005: 16–17.
2   See Dalrymple, 2019 on the rise of the East India Company.

by increased tax revenues. Economic development plans were made and implemented. While Sāmoans were traditionally subsistence gardeners, the Germans sought to establish a progressive, export-led, plantation economy by increasing the land under production, building the labour force and improving agricultural practices. Coconut, cocoa and rubber plantations were greatly expanded and production increased. Sāmoans showed little interest in working for the Germans and DHPG consequently looked offshore for labour. They had recruited a large Melanesian workforce for their plantations prior to 1900 and in 1903 introduced Chinese labourers. By 1914 over 2,000 Chinese were working in German Sāmoa.

Increased production by Sāmoan planters was also encouraged. Landholders were required to plant a minimum number of coconut palms each year, and were given advice on improved agricultural methods. Solf travelled throughout Sāmoa in an effort to understand the country, explain his intentions and build relationships with the leaders.

The German administration had a clear plan; however, the problems they had faced in the 19th century had not disappeared. As colonial historian Jim Davidson[3] noted, '. . . the establishment of satisfactory relations between an alien government and the indigenous people involves far more, in any new colony, than the devising of administrative procedures. In Sāmoa, where the old political structure remained so largely intact and where past relations with foreigners had been so tangled, this problem was one of particular importance and complexity.'[4]

Davidson concluded that 'Solf's approach was essentially paternalistic'. He recognised 'Sāmoan institutions and traditional attitudes only because he saw that to do so was temporarily unavoidable.

3 A New Zealander, James Davidson, Professor of Pacific History at ANU, studied the politics and history of Sāmoa and was intimately involved as a member of the Sāmoan public service, the Legislative Assembly, and as Constitutional Adviser to the Sāmoan Government. His 1967 book, *Sāmoa Mo Sāmoa – The Emergence of the Independent State of Western Sāmoa*, is the work of an academic historian with an insider's knowledge of his subject and is a key reference for this and the following chapter.
4 See Davidson, 1976: 78–79.

His long-term objective was that of breaking them down.' In 1901 Solf wrote: 'The Government's aim must be to get rid of the Central Government in Mulinu'u, this lazy body of intriguers, and to confine the Sāmoan self-government to districts and village.'

Solf had made a careful study of Sāmoan history and politics, informed by the monumental two-volume *The Sāmoa Islands* compiled by ethnologist Dr Augustin Kramer. Early colonial historians[5] gave credit to Solf for his enlightened understanding of and respect for Sāmoan culture. Contemporary Sāmoan historians take a different view of Solf's apparent empathy, sophistication and enlightenment. Malama Meleisea says that Solf used culture to '. . . disguise his long-term intentions. These were to destroy Sāmoan political institutions and replace them with modern rationalised institutions which would consolidate German authority and the expansion of German commercial interests.'[6] Asofou So'o later concluded that 'Solf's aim was to gradually undermine and erode the traditional polity and shift power from the villages and districts to the central administration.'[7] To that end, Solf appointed Tupua Tamasese Titimaea, Tuimaleali'ifano Sualauvi, Saipa'ia and Fa'alata, representatives of the four major paramount titles, as advisers, *Ta'imua*. This 'colonial engineered revision of tradition' recognised *Tama-a-'Āiga* but undermined traditional *pāpā* titles and the *Tafa'ifā*. A Land and Titles Commission,[8] staffed by Europeans, was also established to hear and decide on disputes over land ownership and *matai* titles. Solf selected and appointed Sāmoans, who were loyal to the German regime, as paid government advisers. The Sāmoans provided advice; the Germans made the decisions.

Resistance from Sāmoans came on political and economic fronts. The close relationship between the German government and DHPG, and the preferences given to the European merchants, had kept the price for copra offered to other planters low. This encouraged the

5   For example: Hempenstall, Keesing, Davidson and Firth. Meleisea, 1987: 49.
6   Meleisea, 1987: 50.
7   So'o, 2008: 44.
8   This Commission was the 'German ancestor' of Sāmoa's Land and Titles Court.

small-scale Sāmoan and part-Sāmoan planters to move to form a company, with the support of the *Mālō,* to provide competition to DHPG and improve prices with the profits going to an independent Sāmoan *Mālō.* Solf was opposed to this strategy and instructed the company to cease trading and then regulated against it when the Sāmoans went ahead with their plan. Conflict ensued; *Faipule* and *Pulenu'u* resisting the regulations were imprisoned then broken out of jail when the *Ali'i Sili's* request to free them was declined. The *Ali'i Sili, Ta'imua* and *Faipule* then wrote to the Kaiser in Germany, while Solf was on holiday in New Zealand, expressing dissatisfaction and asking for reforms.

On his return, Solf took Matā'afa Iosefo to task for going to the Kaiser behind his back and strengthened his campaign to undermine the Sāmoan political structure. In August 1905 the *Ta'imua* and *Faipule* were ordered by Solf to leave Mulinu'u and were replaced by a hand-picked, salaried *'Fono of Faipule',* consisting of 27 members carefully chosen by Solf for their loyalty. *Tūmua* and *Pule,* who had asserted they were 'the rulers of Sāmoa', were told that the Germans ruled Sāmoa and that *Tūmua* and *Pule* had no part to play in the German administration.

Solf played off the traditional rivalries within Sāmoa while he got on with the business of building Germany's commercial interests and coconut empire in the Pacific.

Some Sāmoans went along with Solf's regime, particularly those *matai* of lesser rank who were selected for the *Fono of Faipule,* received salaries, and now saw themselves as 'above' other *matai* of higher traditional rank. Solf's interventions upset the balance of power within the traditional Sāmoan cultural hierarchy and led to reaction and opposition from the leaders of Tūmua and Pule.

Lauaki Namulau'ulu Mamoe, who had spoken out publicly for a restoration of the traditional political order as early as 1901, visited Matā'afa Iosefo at Mulinu'u in early 1908. 'Matā'afa wept', Lauaki reported as he told of the ways he had been humiliated by Solf and his authority as *Ali'i Sili* had been diminished. They agreed that the Ta'imua should be restored to office and the role of Tūmua and Pule should be acknowledged. A list of proposals for reform was put together by Lauaki, after consultations with the Taʻimua. The proposals were to be put to Solf when he returned to Sāmoa after his honeymoon in Germany.

Lauaki toured the country speaking to key leaders to gather support and build momentum for greater Sāmoan political independence and participation in governance. But some of the Faipule, including Afamasaga Maua and Teʻo Tuvale who had benefited from government salaries, were unsympathetic and worked to undermine Lauaki by informing their German masters about the growing alliance.[9] They sowed the seeds of factionalism and built resistance against Lauaki and his planned reforms.

In November, Lauaki, against government orders, set out for Mulinuʻu with a fleet of canoes from Savaiʻi. At Leulumoega he discovered that the Āʻana district would not support him and he received another order from the government to return home, this time supported by a letter from Matāʻafa. Defeated, before his proposals had been put to the government, Lauaki returned home to Safotulafai. It was here in December 1908 that Lauaki introduced the term *'Mau a Pule'*, the testimony or opinion of Pule, that would become the motto of the Sāmoan independence movement.

Lauaki Namulauʻulu Mamoe was still an influential leader whose opinion could not be ignored by the German Administration. Solf visited him at Safotulafai, and then summoned Lauaki to Mulinuʻu in January 1909. Accompanied by a canoe fleet of his supporters from Savaiʻi, and allies from Aiga-i-le-Tai, Lauaki made his way to Vaiusu, across the bay from Mulinuʻu, where he was joined by his Tuamāsaga allies. This show of force intimidated Solf who 'forgave Lauaki his past misdeeds and attempted to reach an agreement with him as to the future'. Their differences proved irreconcilable.

Solf demanded the *Fono of Faipule* request Lauaki's deportation and asked for German warships to be sent to Sāmoa to enforce the order. Tensions rose as the Savaiʻi leaders prepared to resist Lauaki's arrest by force and an outbreak of civil war was feared. Missionaries were called in and arranged a peaceful surrender.

9   See Davidson, 1976: 86.

In early 1909, 25-year-old Olaf Frederick Nelson, who we will hear more of later, made a failed attempt to stall Lauaki Namulau'ulu Mamoe's deportation. As a teenager Nelson had met Lauaki at Safune in 1902, and again in 1906. Clearly Lauaki had made an impression on the young Nelson who remembered that 'Lauaki was able by eloquence to draw tears of joy as well as blood'. Nelson had a private meeting in Apia with the Deputy Governor, Dr Schultz, and told him that he '. . . thought Lauaki a great man who was sincere in his intentions for the good of the Sāmoans', and argued that Lauaki would support the Germans, if '. . . he was satisfied that the proper status of the Sāmoan was adequately recognised and reasonable scope was made open for the aspirations of the Sāmoans for the advancement towards self-determination and self-government within a reasonable time'.[10] Nelson failed to change the Germans' mind but his political consciousness was stirred by the fate of Lauaki Namulau'ulu Mamoe.

In March 1909 Lauaki Namulau'ulu Mamoe, with nine of his *matai*, accompanied by family members and a pastor, was taken into exile in the German colony on Saipan in the Mariana Islands, where he would die. For a time *Mau a Pule* was silenced. Lauaki's voice would not be heard again in Sāmoa but his influence on the quest for Sāmoan independence would echo down through the years.

Germany succeeded in driving a wedge between political rivals in Sāmoa. Malietoa Laupepa, Matā'afa Iosefo and Lauaki Namulau'ulu Mamoe were each exiled from Sāmoa. Prior to German rule, Tupua Tamasese Titimaea had been promoted by Governor Solf as King of Sāmoa and was referred to by his rivals as Germany's puppet. Solf favoured the Tamasese clan and encouraged cultural diplomacy through visits of dance troupes to Germany from 1895 and promoting friendships with German-aligned Sāmoan leaders.

With Solf's patronage, Tupua Tamasese Lealofi I travelled to Germany in 1910, accompanied by his wife, Va'aiga, son, Mea'ole, and a troupe of 20 dancers who performed at various 'Zoological Gardens' and festivals throughout Germany. On 26 May 1911, Tamasese met with Kaiser Wilhelm II, presented him with two *'ie*

10 O'Brien, 2017: 26–27.

toga, and 'made a speech expressing the natives' loyalty and devotion'. Dr Solf translated.[11]

Solf left Sāmoa in 1910 and became the German Government's Secretary for The Colonies. He was replaced as Governor of Sāmoa by Dr Erich Schultz, who had been Chief Justice and Chairman of the Land and Titles Commission.

Matā'afa Iosefo died on 12 February 1912 and Schultz, following the recommendation of Solf, abolished the role of *Ali'i Sili,* replacing it with a *Fautua* (Adviser), and appointed Malietoa Tanumafili I and Tupua Tamasese Leolofi I jointly.[12] In making these 'government' appointments, Solf further undermined the traditional roles *tulāfale* played as kingmakers in Sāmoa and demonstrated Germany's power to appoint and anoint Sāmoan leaders sympathetic to Germany.

As the plantation economy expanded, economic growth continued and increased tax revenue funded infrastructural improvements. The German Sāmoan government was stable and the territory became self-supporting; but at what price? Sāmoan political leaders had been reduced to 'advisers' and paid a sinecure, and many European businessmen, part-Sāmoan planters and village farmers struggled with an unfair marketplace, resenting the high taxes. As 1914 dawned, the forces of tradition, ambition and discontent were growing in German Sāmoa. Before they could be expressed or addressed, a larger catastrophe overwhelmed Germany.

11 For an account of Tamasese's visit to Germany see Hilke Thode-Arora, Ed., 2014, *From Sāmoa with Love?*: 173.

12 These appointments prefigured the appointments of Malietoa Tanumafili II and Tupua Tamasese Mea'ole as the joint Head of State of the Independent State of Sāmoa 50 years later.

Chapter 4

New Zealand Administration 1914–1961

New Zealand military forces occupied German Sāmoa during World War I, established military rule and maintained the system of government the German administration had set up. A League of Nations mandate formalised New Zealand's administration of Sāmoa in 1920. In 1945 Sāmoa became a United Nations Trust Territory and New Zealand had the responsibility of 'promoting free political institutions suited to Western Sāmoa'. Throughout the time of the New Zealand Administration Sāmoans continued to press for self-government, it was a rocky 47-year path to independence.

Western Sāmoa

Germany surrendered control of Sāmoa to the New Zealand military at the start of World War I, ending 14 years of German rule and over half a century of German commercial involvement in the economy of Sāmoa and the wider Pacific. New Zealand, a Dominion of the British Empire, took control of Western Sāmoa and Sāmoans' ambition for self-government remained unfulfilled. The United States maintained control of Eastern, American Sāmoa.

Colonial historian Jim Davidson concluded that 'New Zealand control over Western Sāmoa represented the attainment of an old ambition'.[1] From the 1870s New Zealand had repeatedly pressed Great Britain to annex Sāmoa and place it under New Zealand's protection. Politician Sir Robert Stout had been a strong advocate for

---

1   Davidson, 1967: 92. This chapter leans heavily on Davidson. Key quotations are cited in footnotes. To avoid clutter, parenthesis are used for short quotes from Davidson.

British intervention and Premier Richard John Seddon had ambitions for establishing an empire in the South Pacific. Seddon was successful in establishing New Zealand control over Niue, Tokelau and the Cook Islands, but his ambition for Sāmoa was thwarted by the partition of Sāmoa between Germany and the United States of America in 1899. While New Zealand's aspirations had cooled by 1914 they had not been abandoned.

Military Rule 1914–1919

Within days of the outbreak of World War I, a New Zealand expeditionary force landed near Apia, acting on instructions from Great Britain to seize the German radio station in Sāmoa. On 29 August 1914 German Sāmoa was occupied without a shot being fired.

Lieutenant Colonel Robert Logan, leader of the New Zealand military force, raised the Union Jack on 30 August 1914 and declared, on the next day to an assembly of Sāmoans at Mulinu'u, that 'government would be carried on by him on the lines established by the Germans'. Logan became Administrator, as well as military commander, and retained these positions until 1919.

New Zealand military officers and civilians or British residents quickly replaced German officials in Sāmoa.[2] Few of the new officials had the talent, training or qualifications for the positions they found themselves in. Logan, in particular, was ill equipped. Born in Scotland in 1863, Logan came to New Zealand in 1881 and worked as a station hand before buying a sheep run in Otago. He was active in local government and established the Maniototo Mounted Rifle Volunteers in 1900. He joined the regular army, was promoted to Lieutenant Colonel in 1908, made aide-de-camp to the governor general, and then appointed as commander of the Auckland military

2   German citizens were interned in New Zealand. Some families were later repatriated to Germany. Many German men had married Sāmoans and their legacy is found in the names of German–Sāmoan families today. See Tony Brunt's *To Walk Under Palm Trees* for photographs and an account of the lives of German families in Sāmoa and during their internment on Motuihe and Matiu/Somes Islands in New Zealand.

district. In 1915 Logan was promoted to full colonel.

A fifty-one-year-old retired Otago farmer with local government experience, but with no active-duty military service or involvement in 'native' affairs, Logan was called on to run the military and civilian administration of Sāmoa. He had been a 'very capable and excellent District Commander' but was also known to be 'inflexible, unimaginative and authoritarian'.[3] Davidson described Logan's administration as 'ramshackle'. New Zealand's political and military leadership was focused on the war in Europe, sending troops to Egypt, Palestine, Gallipoli and later to the Western Front. Sāmoa was seen as a backwater throughout World War I, was consequently paid little attention and was often sent second-rate or aging soldiers to act as government officials. Wartime conditions also meant stores and goods were in short supply and prices became inflated. However, copra and cocoa remained in demand and achieved good returns throughout the war.

German-owned firms were expropriated by the military administration and liquidated, and export duties were imposed. Chinese and Melanesian labourers were repatriated at the end of their indenture.[4,5] This created difficulties for planters and local businesses; however, some local firms found new opportunities. Foremost was Olaf Frederick Nelson.[6]

Nelson, the son of Swedish trader Auguste Nelson and Sinagogo Masoe, was born in Safune, educated by the Marist Brothers and worked for DHPG before joining his father's firm in 1900. He established his own firm in 1903 and later absorbed his father's. Though his mother was Sāmoan, Nelson enjoyed European status through his Swedish father. Later he would become a British subject, and this status enabled him to avoid the restrictions that 'Native Sāmoans'

3 Munro, 1996.
4 Chinese married to Sāmoans were allowed to remain and their legacy is found in Chinese–Sāmoan families today.
5 A small group of Melanesian labourers were never returned. Malama Meleisea's 1980 account, *'O Tama Uli – Melanesians in Sāmoa*, tells their story.
6 See Wendt, 1965, Laracy, 1998, and O'Brien, 2012, who has written a full biography of Nelson.

faced under German and later New Zealand Administrations. Following the expulsion of German traders, Nelson took over many of their stores and inter-island vessels, and the copra trade that they were forced to abandon, establishing a near monopoly. Nelson profited from the high copra prices during World War I, becoming wealthy and influential in Sāmoa.

Military rule was reluctantly accepted by Sāmoans until disaster hit on 7 November 1918, four days before the end of World War I. On that day the ship *Talune* arrived in Apia harbour with passengers carrying pneumonic influenza. Quarantine restrictions were not imposed and an incompetent administration compounded the situation by not restricting internal travel, allowing the epidemic to spread throughout Sāmoa.

The 'Spanish Flu' was a global phenomenon, exacerbated by troops returning home. New Zealand suffered 5,471 deaths, 0.5% of the population, which was considered 'heavy'; but Sāmoa lost an estimated 8,500 people, 22% of the population – the largest recorded percentage of population loss through an epidemic of any nation. Many people were buried in mass graves and traditional funeral protocols were set aside as the magnitude of the disaster overwhelmed the capacity of the government and village communities to respond. Few families escaped unscathed; many families lost most of their members. Nelson lost his mother, his only brother and his wife, one of his two sisters, and his young son. This tragedy embittered Nelson against the New Zealand administration.

As Sāmoans slowly recovered from the grief of their losses they looked for the reasons why the epidemic had such a devastating impact on Sāmoa. New Zealand's military administration became the focus of the blame. A commission of enquiry was convened by the New Zealand Government and visited Sāmoa in mid-1919. Jim Davidson, who first visited Sāmoa less than 30 years after the epidemic, wrote that the Commission was 'thorough', and though the report told an appalling story, its conclusions were 'fair-minded'.[7]

The report found that the *Talune,* on its voyage from Auckland,

7   Davidson, 1967: 95.

had been informed that pneumonic influenza was a notifiable disease, but the administration in Sāmoa had not been informed. The *Talune* called in to the Fijian ports of Suva and Levuka where the ship had been quarantined, but the captain had not informed the Apia Port Medical Officer of the risk and passengers had been able to disembark, even though some were clearly unwell. American Sāmoa had avoided the disease by the Governor imposing a strict quarantine, and, during the height of the epidemic, he had offered to send medical assistance to Apia. Logan turned down the offer and ordered a temporary cessation of radio communications with Pago Pago because he was angry that the mail from Western Sāmoa had also been quarantined. While there were individual acts of kindness and compassion, there were many examples of 'folly and confusion' in the administration of health services, including closure of hospitals and a lack of travel restrictions unwittingly spreading the disease throughout Sāmoa.

The epidemic had an uneven impact. There was a particularly high death rate amongst older *matai,* with a subsequent loss of knowledge and disruption of traditional political activity resulting in a shift to a new generation of political leaders who had little faith in New Zealand's administration of Sāmoa. Davidson concludes his account of the influenza epidemic by stating: '. . . in truth, the poor quality of administration had been exposed in a way that none who witnessed the exposure would ever forget . . .' and: 'The epidemic, while weakening the forces of an older traditionalism, has provided the people with a new reason for resentment of the administering authority; and such resentment is one of the classic bases of colonial nationalism.'

The consequences of the 1918 influenza epidemic were far-reaching. Logan's military administration was ended, New Zealand woke up to its responsibility, and a new generation of more assertive Sāmoan leaders began to challenge New Zealand's administration of Sāmoa and push for self-government.

The Mandate 1920–1945

The Peace Conference in Paris, following the end of World War I, started the process of determining the fate of former German territories and possessions and establishing the League of Nations. It was clear that this process would take some time and delay any formal mandate in Sāmoa. In the meantime, the New Zealand Government introduced legislation to Parliament to establish a civil administration in Sāmoa. The parliamentary debate soon exposed the positions of the major political parties.

The ruling Reform Party of Prime Minister William Massey followed the established conservative line that Sāmoa was important for New Zealand's defence, should remain a New Zealand territory, be economically self-supporting, and be administered as part of New Zealand's Civil Service. This position was supported by the opposition Liberal Party.[8] The only dissent was from the recently elected Labour Party Members of Parliament, Harry Holland and Peter Fraser, who advocated for internal self-government under international supervision. They said that Sāmoans were capable of self-government, attacked the continued use of indentured labour and said the government was not establishing a democracy but a form of autocracy. The Labour position was prescient but ignored.

The New Zealand Parliament considered two bills to formalise the governance of Sāmoa. The first would create a Department of External Affairs, to control Sāmoa and other dependencies, and the second, the Samoa Constitution Order, to provide the basic law and incorporate a number of New Zealand statutes. Under these laws, executive power would be the responsibility of a New Zealand–appointed Administrator, and legislative power vested in a Legislative Council of officials, with a minority of three unofficial members representing the European community. The existing Fono of Faipule would remain, but without legal recognition or any authority. There was a brief consultation in Sāmoa on the proposal in which the

8 Davidson considered this view 'naïve, ill-informed and out-dated'. Davidson, 1967: 95.

Fono of Faipule and a Citizens Committee, chaired by O.F. Nelson, presented their objections and lists of requests for greater Sāmoan participation. No concessions were made and, after the mandate from the League of Nations was confirmed in December 1920, *The Sāmoa Act (1921)* came into effect on 1 April 1922. It would remain the basic law for 40 years, with some amendments, until independence.

Once again, an occupying power had put in place instruments of governance and appointed governors without Sāmoan participation. Sāmoans objected and the Fono of Faipule directly petitioned King George V seeking self-government, but was ignored. Paternalist control of Sāmoa would continue for the next two decades.

Colonel Robert Ward Tate, a solicitor in private life, who was Acting Administrator after Logan's demise, was appointed his successor. Tate was a modest, quiet man whose three years in charge was characterised by inactivity. He was replaced in March 1923 by Major-General Sir George Spafford Richardson.[9] Richardson was a man of drive, energy and ambition that had led to his success as a field officer in the Gallipoli campaign and on the Western Front, and resulted in a number of senior military appointments, including commanding all New Zealand troops in the United Kingdom. He brought this energy and administrative skill to his role as Administrator of Sāmoa but he also had a paternalistic attitude, never developed more than a superficial understanding of Sāmoan society, and was indifferent towards Sāmoan political traditions.

Richardson vigorously pursued a series of reforms and developments to: 'promote the welfare of the Native Race' through addressing the principal 'Native Problems', namely: 1. Health. How to make the Sāmoan Race a healthy, strong and increasing one. 2. Education. How to ensure that the education of the Natives harmonises with their surroundings and future requirements so as to maintain their happiness and contentment. 3. Economic. How to get the Natives to make fuller use of their lands, and to increase production.[10]

To implement his reforms and gain Sāmoan support, Richardson

9   McGibbon, 1996.
10 Richardson's own words cited by Davidson, 1967: 104.

worked to involve the Fono of Faipule, his hand-picked forum of senior *matai*. Legal representation was established through the *Sāmoa Amendment Act 1923*, and Richardson used committees of Faipule to advise him. The Fono of Faipule could also make regulations through the *Native Regulations (Sāmoa) Order 1925*. Districts, represented by Faipule and controlled by District Councils, were established with local officials, *pulenu'u*, to control all local matters. Village committees could establish local rules and enforce orders issued by the Government and District Councils. Women's Committees were established in villages to work with the Department of Health to improve hygiene and medical care. This form of local government was built on the foundation of village governance that had been in place for hundreds of years, but was now part of a centrally controlled hierarchy of governance with village councils at the bottom, district councils next, under a Department of Native Affairs, with the Governor at the top.

Some villages responded positively and rebuilt their communities on the new model, improving sanitation and constructing new houses. *Faletalimālō* of *matai*, sited in front of family residences, were arranged in a circle around a village *malae* where the *faletele* of the high chief was placed. The village of Lepea on the outskirts of Apia, smartly painted in blue and white, still reflects the formal 'army camp' style that Richardson promoted. Unfortunately, a busy main road now cuts across the village green.

Richardson had a grand plan: a place for everything and everything (and everybody) in its place. His military training, administrative experience and great energy were focused on achieving the goals he had set. However, success in governance requires more than a plan; it requires the 'governor' gaining the hearts and minds of the 'governed' and taking the people with him. Participation and partnership were not part of Richardson's governance vocabulary. Colonial paternalism had failed in the recent past and would fail again. Sāmoans' desire for greater involvement in their own governance, on their own terms, led to resistance and an unravelling of Richardson's reforms. Land tenure would become the focus of this resistance.

Richardson was aware of the large area of uncultivated land in

Sāmoa and saw its development as a key to improving agriculture and strengthening economic self-sufficiency. He admired the Tongan system of landholding and sent a delegation of Faipule to Tonga to study the system. On the delegation's return, a plan was developed and adopted by the Fono of Faipule. The idea was for District Councils to divide and allocate land, providing a lifetime leasehold title and charging an annual rental for selected participants. Effectively, the Government was taking over control of land previously controlled by the village *fono*. This new system ran in direct opposition to the Sāmoan practice where *matai* had stewardship of land linked to their titles. Sāmoan resistance grew.

Sāmoans of influence, many who had learnt to speak English, bridled against the colonial paternalism. These notably included: Tupua Tamasese Lealofi III, who had earlier travelled to Germany with his father and was well educated by the Marist Brothers; Matā'afa Faumuinā Fiame Mulinu'u, who had married the daughter of Malietoa Laupepa; and Afamasaga Toleafoa Lagolago. The latter two were businessmen; all had senior *matai* titles and operated successfully in both the Sāmoan and Palagi worlds. They would soon become leaders of the resistance.

The elected members of the Legislative Council also pushed back against the Administrator. The three European members, elected under a property franchise, were wealthy traders. Two were married to Sāmoan women and the third, Olaf Frederick Nelson, had 'European' status through his Swedish father but was proudly Sāmoan and held the chiefly titles Toleafoa and Ta'isi. Nelson was a wealthy man, an international traveller who was entertained by Lloyd George when he visited London, and lived and entertained in high style in Sāmoa. He became a symbol of aspiration for young Sāmoans. This did not go down well with Richardson or the expatriate officials who ruled with an assumption of authority. While there were good intentions, there was an undercurrent of white superiority in New Zealand's relationship with Sāmoa and Sāmoans. Richardson's patronising attitude is reflected in his statement: 'Here in Sāmoa is a splendid but backward Native race . . .'[11]

The stage was set for a confrontation between a patronising and inflexible New Zealand administration and Sāmoans seeking greater participation in the governance of their homeland, resources and people. Richardson and Nelson would become the central figures in the impending confrontation.

In September 1926, Nelson returned to Sāmoa after a lengthy trip to Australia and New Zealand. In Wellington, Nelson had met with the Prime Minister, Gordon Coates, and the Minister of External Affairs, William Nosworthy, setting out local grievances against the New Zealand Administration, and asking Nosworthy to investigate them on his planned October visit to Sāmoa. This was agreed. In preparation for the Minister's visit, Nelson organised a series of public meetings of the Citizens' Committee of Europeans and Sāmoans to draft a list of complaints and requests, and elect representatives to meet with Nosworthy. Worried by these developments, Richardson informed the first public meeting that the Minister's visit would be delayed by six months. The second meeting, keen to make progress and concerned of further delaying tactics, resolved to send a delegation to meet the Minister in New Zealand. Richardson raised the stakes, believing this was the action of a small group of malcontents, and refused to issue passports to delegates and passed a bill at the Legislative Council making it an offence to advocate civil disobedience and spread false information about the government.

Rather than reducing tensions, Richardson's actions sparked organised resistance by Sāmoans, echoing Lauaki's oratory and actions a generation earlier. One of the intended delegates, S.H. Meredith, took himself off to New Zealand to meet Nosworthy and publicise the Sāmoan grievances. The Citizens' Committee drafted a petition setting out the grievances and sought signatures to show that the complaints were widespread and Nelson founded a newspaper, the *Samoa Guardian*, in opposition to the pro-government *Samoa Times*. Then, in March 1927, 'The Samoan League' was established, named in the Sāmoan language *'O le Mau*, honouring Lauaki's vision

11 Cited by Davidson, 1967: 112.

of collective action for independent Sāmoan governance.

In June Nosworthy arrived in Sāmoa. His visit was a disaster. He had been briefed by Richardson and accepted his analysis of the situation. Nosworthy's programme was carefully stage-managed to avoid the large numbers of *Mau* supporters gathered in Apia. Towards the end of his visit Nosworthy finally met the Citizens' Committee. Rather than listening to the Sāmoans and forming his own opinion, he sided with the Administration. He tactlessly labelled the European members 'self-serving intriguers', suggested that Nelson's lifestyle was 'aping the Governor' and said that the law would be amended to enable the Administration to deport 'disaffected' Europeans (including part-Europeans). This comment was clearly targeted at Nelson.

On Nosworthy's departure, resistance hardened as Richardson escalated the situation by issuing a proclamation for the *Mau* to disband and threatening punishment of those 'advising or suggesting any disobedience'.

Many Europeans felt it was unsafe to publicly support the work of the *Mau*, but Nelson and A.G. Smythe went to New Zealand to support the Sāmoan petition to Parliament, while Sāmoan leaders stayed in Apia awaiting developments. Richardson responded by banishing Faumuinā and Afamasaga to the island of Apolima and punished many other *matai*. These actions strengthened the resolve of the *Mau*, recruited many more Sāmoans to the cause of '*Sāmoa mo Sāmoa*', and led to a country-wide campaign of civil disobedience and non-cooperation with the Administration.

New Zealand took notice. A Royal Commission was appointed on 12 September 1927 '. . . to conduct an independent and impartial inquiry into the complaints against the Administration'. Sir Charles Skerrett, Chief Justice of New Zealand, was chairman and C.E. McCormick, Judge of the New Zealand Native Land Court, was the other member. They travelled to Sāmoa to hear and cross-examine witnesses and gather evidence.

The Royal Commission reported to the Governor-General on 29 November 1927. The report was a whitewash: '. . . it concluded that the complaints were without foundation. It dismissed the charge that Richardson had acted without "due regard to the customs and feelings of the people of Sāmoa"; and affirmed the justice and propriety of his policy in regard to the Faipule and his exercise of the powers of banishment'.[12] The Commissioners took a narrow legalistic approach, were highly critical of the evidence provided by the Citizens' Committee and the *Mau*, and accepted Richardson's view '. . . that the *Mau* was largely the product of intrigue by a few unscrupulous and ambitious men, under Nelson's domination'. The Commissioners lacked any real understanding of Sāmoan society and ignored the longstanding concerns of the majority of Sāmoans who supported the *Mau*.

Richardson held firm and, shortly after the Commission's conclusions were released, deported Nelson and E.W. Gurr, Editor of the *Samoa Guardian*, for five years, and A.G. Smythe for two years. Nelson, fearing a violent uprising, left Sāmoa voluntarily after meeting with the *Mau* urging it to disperse. However, civil disobedience continued and members of the *Mau* paraded through Apia in uniform, picketing Government agencies, refusing to pay taxes, and undermining the Government. Most of the police were Sāmoans and were reluctant to enforce the law. Richardson, fearing a complete breakdown of authority, quickly passed a law to forbid the wearing of *Mau* uniforms and raising funds for political activity, and asked the New Zealand Government to send two navy cruisers and marines, echoing the German and British 'naval justice' tactics of the 19th century. When the Navy arrived, the marines arrested and jailed 400 members of the *Mau*. Hundreds more asked to be arrested and insisted on being dealt by the courts and then rejected its jurisdiction. This strategy of passive resistance made a farce of the law as the Government could not handle the numbers. Tupua Tamasese Lealofi III, as the spokesman of the *Mau*, insisted that their objective was self-government.

Richardson's five-year term in office ended in April 1928. He had been welcomed with high expectations but departed in failure and ridicule. His successor was Colonel Stephen Shepherd Allen, a

---

12 See: Report of the Royal Commission concerning the Administration of Western Sāmoa, 1927, cited by Davidson, 167: 129.

Cambridge University graduate in mathematics and law and a farmer and lawyer. In contrast to Richardson, he did not enjoy public events and speech making, soon gaining the nickname 'Silent Steve'.

With Nelson in exile in New Zealand, Tupua Tamasese Lealofi III assumed leadership of the *Mau* and built up its administrative capacity and structure. A petition to the League of Nations that set out grievances was signed by 85% (7,982 of 9,325) of Sāmoan tax-payers. The *Mau* reasserted Sāmoan traditionalism with senior orators of Tūmua and Pule amongst the leadership, which now included the paramount chief Tuimaleali'ifano Fa'aloi'i, who was consequently dismissed as a Fautua. The *Mau* had become the dominant political force in Sāmoa in contrast to a small minority of dissidents and government office holders.

Allen, following Richardson's lead, was convinced that the *Mau* would slowly fade away and that firm police action would encourage the decline. The New Zealand Police arrested tax defaulters and many *Mau* supporters fled into the bush and were concealed by their families. In November 1928 Tamasese was arrested and convicted of non-payment of tax and resisting the police. There was a violent clash between the police and *Mau* supporters. Tamasese was sent to New Zealand and imprisoned. In the meantime, Nelson had attempted to present a petition to the League of Nations Mandates Commission in Geneva but was not permitted. He returned to Sāmoa, published the *New Zealand Samoa Guardian* newspaper and formed the New Zealand Samoan Defence League to advance the cause. New Zealand newspapers reported events in Sāmoa and Nelson cultivated the support of the New Zealand Labour Party.

At the end of 1928, Coates' Reform Party Government was defeated at the general election and replaced by a United Party Government led by Sir Joseph Ward, with the support of Labour. This led to some modifications of the administration of Sāmoa. Malietoa Tanumafili and Matā'afa Salanoa, supporters of the Government, were appointed by Allen as Fautua and members of the Legislative Council. During 1929 low-level agitation and demonstrations by the *Mau* against the Government continued.

In June 1929, Tamasese returned to Sāmoa, amongst mass

celebrations, and in November Tuimaleali'ifano and Faumuinā returned from their visit to New Zealand encouraged by the support they had received. A major reception was planned for the return of A.G. Smyth from his two-year exile. Allen's 'softly softly' approach had appeared to relax tensions, but this lull proved to be the calm before the storm.

Black Saturday

Early on Saturday 28 December 1929, a procession that had received police permission set out down Beach Road heading towards the wharf to welcome Smyth. As the procession paused to salute the Union Jack, on display at the Central Office building, the police moved in and attempted to arrest the *Mau* Secretary Mata'utia Kaauna, and a scuffle broke out. A policeman fell over and nervous members of the arresting party, armed with revolvers, opened fire on the procession. They were quickly joined by a machine gun firing from the police station. The leaders of the *Mau*, Tamasese, Faumuinā and Tuimalieali'ifano, called for calm. Eleven Sāmoans, mostly senior *matai*, died, including Tupua Tamasese Lealofi III. His final recorded words were: 'My blood has been spilt for Sāmoa. I am proud to give it. Do not dream of avenging it, as it was spilt maintaining peace. If I die, peace must be maintained at any price.'

The tragic events on Black Saturday[13] would echo down through the years and prove to be a harbinger of Sāmoan independence.

Pressure by the Government on the *Mau* continued in the weeks that followed. Allen pledged to maintain law and order, declared the *Mau* to be a seditious organisation, acted to crush protests, and worked to bankrupt Nelson through harsh taxation. Members of the *Mau* fled to the bush. A naval cruiser was called up from New Zealand. Police, marines and an aeroplane searched the bush for members of the *Mau*, restrictions were placed on travel, and villages were searched by armed men at night. Stories of violence and brutality are told of

---

13 Much has been written on the events and consequences of Black Saturday and the Mau. See: Field, 1984, 2006; Meleisea, 1987; O'Brien, 2017.

this time, as the New Zealanders attempted to break the organisation and spirit of the *Mau*.

The New Zealand Minister of Defence, J.G. Cobbe, came to Sāmoa and arranged an amnesty so that formal talks and a settlement could be organised with the *Mau*. But Allen was resolute and demanded the dissolution of the *Mau* and the surrender of all of those wanted by the police. Faumuinā, now the spokesman for the *Mau*, agreed that those wanted by the police should surrender themselves but maintained that 'Sāmoa is the *Mau*' and the objective of self-government remained the priority. The situation gradually calmed down and the naval cruiser, the aeroplane and the marines returned to New Zealand. Allen declared that he had broken the *Mau*. The Fono of Faipule was reinstated but was boycotted by the *Mau*. The imprisoned leaders, on their release, returned to their villages and continued organising for independence. Allen, naïvely, did not appreciate some Sāmoans' capacity to say one thing and do another, with smiles on their faces.

In April 1931, Allen completed his term as Administrator and returned to New Zealand, replaced by Brigadier General Herbert Ernest Hart, another in the line of country solicitor turned soldier selected to administer Sāmoa. The *Mau* continued low-level, non-violent action, and the Administration continued to act against 'illegal' activity such as the wearing of *Mau* uniforms and the organisation of unsanctioned processions. Petitions continued to be sent to the governments of Great Britain, the United States, Germany and New Zealand, and to the League of Nations, seeking Sāmoan self-government.

On 16 May 1933 Nelson returned to Apia. Hart considered Nelson a European and wanted to meet him in an attempt to negotiate a settlement, but would not accept him as a Sāmoan representative of the *Mau*. Negotiations never started. The *Mau* considered the New Zealand Government an outside imposition on Sāmoa's sovereignty, a view held since the time of Lauaki Namulauʻulu Mamoe, and continued working towards establishing an independent Sāmoan government in opposition to the New Zealand Administration.

The proposed autonomous 'government' included prominent traditional chiefs, including: Tuimalealiʻifano; Tupua Tamasese

Mea'ole (who had succeeded Tupua Tamasese Lealofi III and in 1934 had married Nelson's daughter, consolidating a family commitment to the *Mau*); and Faumuinā as President of the *Mau*. A 'constitution' was prepared and plans were made for the future government. Nelson worked quietly on the administrative arrangements and funded much of the work including sponsoring *malaga* throughout Sāmoa to gather support. There were always tensions, jealousies and personal ambitions within the membership of the *Mau*. The Inspector of Police, A.L. Braisby, maintained a network of informers within the *Mau*. Their information led to Police raids and fourteen *malaga* members were arrested and imprisoned for a year. Nelson was also arrested, for supporting a 'seditious' organisation, and sentenced to eight months jail and ten years' exile from Sāmoa.

Nelson sailed into exile on the *Maui Pomare*, ironically named after his friend, the Māori Member of Parliament. One of his last acts before leaving Sāmoa was to write an article, for what was to be the final issue of the *New Zealand Samoa Guardian,* reflecting on his meeting with Lauaki Namulau'ulu Mamoe in 1909, his own exile now repeating Lauaki's, and the fact that they were both now looked upon as 'rebels' rather than 'patriots'.[14] Nelson's exile was short and, unlike Lauaki Namulau'ulu Mamoe, he returned to Sāmoa. The attempt to form an autonomous 'government' was foiled; but the tide of history was turning.

The Tide Turns

In 1935 the New Zealand Labour Party, led by Michael Joseph Savage, swept into government signalling a dramatic change in the New Zealand Government's relationship with Sāmoa. Savage met with Nelson and told him that his exile would soon end and a 'goodwill mission' was to be sent to Sāmoa. The Minister of Lands, Frank Langstone, and James O'Brien MP were welcomed in Apia by Malietoa and a large procession of *Mau* members. Langston announced that the Government would repeal the proclamation that the *Mau* was a

14 O'Brien, 2017: 276.

seditious organisation and held a series of meetings discussing reform. Nelson returned to Sāmoa amidst great celebrations and the following day Langston announced proposals: to repeal the Sāmoan Offenders Ordinance; write off tax levies; increase the Sāmoan membership of the Legislative Council; establish a Finance Committee; select a new Fono of Faipule; appoint a Sāmoan associate judge to sit in the High Court; and increase the number of local people in the Public Service. Whilst these proposals dealt with current grievances, and were accepted as sign of goodwill, they fell short of self-government.

'The *Mau* were triumphant', and they won 33 of the 39 seats on the new Fono of Faipule. Faumuinā was appointed Supervisor of Native Police and Tupua Tamasese Mea'ole took over as President of the *Mau*. Tuimaleali'ifano was appointed as Fautua following the death of Matā'afa Salanoa. There was a feeling that real change had come. However, disappointment would soon follow as the senior government officials that the *Mau* had asked to be removed remained in place and stalled reforms.

When Hart's term ended in 1935, the Administration's Secretary, Alfred Clarke Turnbull, was appointed Acting Administrator until 1943, when he was confirmed as Administrator. Turnbull was an 'old school' colonial official and 'servant of Wellington'. His uncertain tenure, lack of imagination and lack of sympathy for Sāmoans resulted in him being 'despised and ignored'. The European planters also resisted change, resenting the decision to stop the import of Chinese indentured labourers, and formed a political party to defend their interests. While the political climate in Wellington had shifted, there was no real change in European attitudes in Apia.

Meanwhile, the *Mau* maintained their long-term objective of self-government and a new generation took over leadership. The *Mau* continued to push for greater Sāmoan participation in the governance of Sāmoa, proposing that Nelson be appointed to the Fono of Faipule as *Fa'atonu* and as a Sāmoan representative on the Legislative Council. Disagreements continued between Turnbull and the *Mau* over policies and appointments, and in 1938 a delegation, led by Nelson and Tamasese and financed by the *Mau*, went to Wellington to speak directly to Prime Minister Savage. 'Savage – a master of the soothing phrase . . .' impressed the delegation with his friendliness and they abandoned some of their demands.[15] Once again, New Zealand's priorities had trumped Sāmoa's ambitions.

Sāmoa marked time as the generations changed and the Government in New Zealand was increasingly distracted by rumours of war in Europe and Asia. Central government in Sāmoa was essentially ceremonial and had a limited impact on the lives of most Sāmoans who lived in their village communities governed by *fono matai*. The 100-year-old Tuimaleali'ifano Fa'aoloi'i died in 1937 and was replaced by Tupua Tamasese Mea'ole as Fautua, and two years later Malietoa Tanumafili died and was replaced by Malietoa Tanumafili II. Matā'afa Faumuinā Fiamē was appointed the third Fautua in 1943. Olaf Frederick Nelson's health deteriorated, exacerbated by his time spent in exile and the loss of much of his fortune, and he died in 1944.

Meanwhile, in 1942 American forces, responding to the Imperial Japanese Navy's attack on Pearl Harbour in Hawaii, arrived in Apia and set up camp in preparation for the war in the Pacific and the invasion of Japan. The Sāmoan economy started to grow again, following the low commodity prices and the global economic depression of the 1930s. Copra and cocoa were in demand and the American presence stimulated the local economy. Peter Fraser had become prime minister of New Zealand following the death of Michael Joseph Savage in 1941. He visited Sāmoa in 1944 and listened to Sāmoan grievances. While wartime austerity limited his actions, he did set up a scholarship scheme for talented Sāmoan children to go to New Zealand for further education, and appointed a new Administrator, Lieutenant Colonel Francis William Voelcker. Voelcker had been a successful commander of Pacific Island troops in Fiji and the Solomon Islands and had empathy for the Pacific.

As the war in the Pacific came to an end, Sāmoa was still, constitutionally, far from self-government. But the tide had turned. A new generation of Sāmoan leaders had emerged, New Zealanders' attitudes were changing, and there was an international appetite

15 Davidson, 1967: 154.

for change following the horrors of World War II. In his Inaugural Address, American President Harry Truman captured the mood of the times and set out a four-point plan for post-war development.

> In the coming years, our program for peace and freedom will emphasize four major courses of action. First, we will continue to give unfaltering support to the United Nations . . . and we will continue to search for ways to strengthen their authority and increase their effectiveness. We believe that the United Nations will be strengthened by the new nations which are being formed in lands now advancing toward self-government under democratic principles. Second, we will continue our programs for world economic recovery . . . Third, we will strengthen freedom-loving nations against the dangers of aggression . . . Fourth, we must embark on a bold new program for making the benefits of our scientific advances and industrial progress available for the improvement and growth of underdeveloped areas. The old imperialism, exploitation for foreign profit, has no place in our plans. What we envisage is a program of development based on the concepts of democratic fair-dealing . . .[16]

Truman's statement is often cited as marking the end of the era of colonisation by European and Asian imperial powers and the beginning of a new era of decolonisation, development, modernisation and the establishment of independent, self-governing nations in Asia, Africa and the Pacific. In 1947, India led the way, and now Sāmoa was starting down the path that would lead to independence in 1962.

Trusteeship 1945–1961

Peter Fraser had chaired the committee on trusteeships during the conference that drafted the Charter of the United Nations in 1945. In early 1946 he invited the Legislative Council and the Fautua to discuss a draft agreement for placing Sāmoa under United Nations trusteeship.

16 See: Truman, 1949.

The Sāmoans requested a wider discussion, and on 13 November a 'Fono of All Sāmoa' met at Mulinu'u. Fraser sent Foss Shanahan, Assistant Secretary of External Affairs, to explain the purpose of a trusteeship to the Fono, and then he and the Administrator withdrew to allow the Sāmoans to discuss the proposal. For the first time, the leaders of Sāmoa had been invited to participate in an open-ended discussion among themselves about the future shape of the governance of Sāmoa, without the presence and direction of an occupying power.

Many Sāmoans wanted immediate self-government and were suspicious of the 'Trust Territory' status; others argued for a gradual move towards political independence, with time and training to build the capacity for self-government; yet others argued in favour of United States control and reuniting with American Sāmoa.[17] The Fono went on for five days and eventually the text of a letter to the Administrator was agreed as 'the freely expressed wishes of the Sāmoan people' to be presented by New Zealand to the United Nations. The key clauses were: '1. We humbly beseech that Sāmoa be granted self-government. 2. We earnestly pray that New Zealand will see fit to act as Protector and adviser to Sāmoa . . .' The Administrator agreed to the Fono's request.

On 13 December 1946, the United Nations General Assembly approved the trustee agreement with 'Western Sāmoa'. In March 1947, the Trusteeship Council began its first session and New Zealand presented the Sāmoan petition and asked that an investigation be undertaken in the matters the petition raised. The Trusteeship Council appointed a special mission to visit Western Sāmoa chaired by Francis B. Sayre, President of the Trusteeship Council and son-in-law of former United States President Woodrow Wilson, Pierre Ryckmans, former Governor General of the Belgian Congo, and Eduardo Cruz-Coke, member of the Chilean Senate and professor of the Santiago Medical School. Jim Davidson[18] and George Laking

17 Around 90% wanted an end of the partition from American Sāmoa and transfer to US control, but the US was not interested. Davidson, 1976: 166.
18 Davidson, who went on the write *Sāmoa mo Sāmoa, the Emergence of the Independent State of Western Sāmoa*, 1967, had an insider's view of the UN mission and would later have a key role in the writing of the Sāmoan Constitution and developments leading to independence.

were appointed by Fraser to be the New Zealand External Affairs Department's representatives to accompany the UN mission.

Davidson formed a close relationship with Cruz-Coke, who insisted that the Fautua, who were accepted by Sāmoans as their rightful leaders, should have a role at the highest level of government. Davidson and Laking met privately with the Fautua to discuss constitutional changes and build trust as the first steps were put in place for eventual self-government. Before the UN mission reported, the New Zealand Government moved to put in place a series of constitutional changes including: adopting the term 'the Government of Western Sāmoa' in place of the 'Administration of Sāmoa'; replacing the 'Administrator' with a 'High Commissioner'; establishing a 'Council of State', consisting of the High Commissioner and the Fautua; replacing the Legislative Council with a 'Legislative Assembly' with full powers and a Sāmoan majority; and establishing an 'Independent Public Service'. These, and other policy changes, which were 'intended to confer added dignity and to give substance to New Zealand's acceptance of Western Sāmoa as a self-governing state in the making', were incorporated into a draft Samoa Amendment Bill that was taken to Sāmoa for consultation with the Fautua. The UN mission's report was published in September and the findings were consistent with the bill. In November The Samoa Amendment Act, 1947, was passed by both houses of Parliament and brought into force by proclamation on 10 March 1948.

Prime Minister Fraser had moved quickly because he knew that his time in office would be limited and was unsure if his successor would show the same commitment to moving Sāmoa towards self-government. He was right on the first count, as Labour was defeated in 1949, but wrong on the second count, as successive New Zealand governments accepted that the political future of Western Sāmoa would be planned in Apia not Wellington.

Seumanutafa Pogai, High Chief of Apia village, was the first point of contact for foreigners arriving in Apia harbour.

Malietoa Laupepa was a central figure in the contested governance of Sāmoa during the second half of the 19th century.

Matā'afa Iosefo was chosen to succeed Malietoa Laupepa as Sāmoa's leader, based on 'culture and tradition', and backed by Lauaki Namulau'ulu Mamoe.

Tupua Tamasese Titimaea, installed as 'King of Sāmoa' in 1887 by German political and commercial interests, backed up by German Navy gunships.

Matā'afa Iosefo, and ten of his prominent supporters, were exiled on Jaluit Atoll in the German-ruled Marshall Islands.

Tupua Tamasese Lealofi I and Solf in Berlin, where they met Kaiser Wilhelm II in 1911.

Hooray! Sāmoa is Ours! German poster, 1899, celebrating German governance of Sāmoa.

Constitutional Convention, 1960.

Constitutional Convention in Session: Jim Davidson, Tupua Tamasese
Meaole, Malietoa Tanumafili II, Colin Aikman.

Malietoa Tanumafili II and Tupua Tamasese Meaole
raising the Sāmoan flag on 1 January 1962.

Unconstitutional swearing-in ceremony, 2021.

Former Head of State at the unconstitutional swearing-in ceremony.

Police blockade of HRPP MPs from Parliament.

Tuila'epa addresses crowd outside Parliament.

The Chief Justice and members of the Judiciary, accompanied by Police, head to Parliament Buildings.

Tuilaʻepa leads HRPP MPs into Parliament to be sworn in.

Chapter 5

Achieving Independence

Under the mandate of the United Nations, Western Sāmoa took a gradual path towards self-government. Constitutional Conventions were convened, laws drafted, new democratic institutions were established, and Sāmoans were elected and appointed to leadership positions. A conversation, aimed at achieving a balance between customary leadership and democratic governance, resolved the key concerns of Sāmoans, led to a unique constitution for the Independent State of Western Sāmoa and ultimately the termination of the United Nations' Trusteeship Agreement.

Preparing for Self-Government

In the years following World War II independence from colonial rule was achieved by many new nations in Africa, Asia, the Middle East, the Caribbean, South America and across the Pacific. Relinquishing colonial control was never easy. The historian Norman Davies wrote, 'The truest words on this subject were spoken between Gertrude Bell and a prominent Iraqi official. "Britain aims to give Iraq complete independence," said Gertrude. "My lady," replied Jafar Pasha Al-Askari, "complete independence is never given; it is always taken."'[1]

Some nations fought for their freedom, others took the path of gradual change. Some colonial powers resisted change, others simply walked away, and yet others worked as partners in facilitating a change in governance. Whether self-government was achieved by revolution or evolution, the process of change had consequences for the political, social and economic development of newly emerging nations. For

---

1 Davies, 2018: 641.

some, the trauma of the struggle for independence took years to heal, for others the process was smoother and the outcome more peaceful. A few territories remain under colonial control.

Western Sāmoa and New Zealand chose gradualism and trod a relatively even and peaceful path towards self-government. In 1949, before the United Nations Trusteeship Council's mission to Sāmoa had reported, the New Zealand Government had put in place the steps that would lead to Sāmoa's self-government. During the 1950s Western Sāmoa moved steadily towards political independence as the capacity of local people and new institutions were built to manage the mechanics of the independent governance of Sāmoa. The path to political independence was not always smooth. While the political leaders were clear on their aims, some of the expatriate public servants were slow or reluctant to make way for locals, and some of the locals were impatient with the slow rate of change. Furthermore, improving the economic development of Sāmoa was necessary to provide financial support for the emerging independent nation and required political certainty. Steady leadership was essential during this time of change.

One of the most significant figures in shaping the path to independence was Guy Richardson Powles,[2] who arrived in Sāmoa on 1 March 1949 to take up his role as High Commissioner. Powles was a lawyer who had held a senior military rank and seen active service in the Pacific during World War II. He joined the Department of External Affairs, was seconded to the Prime Minister's Department and served in the New Zealand Legation in Washington, DC. As a member of the Far Eastern Advisory Commission, he visited Japan in 1946 and was deeply affected by the atomic bomb's devastation of Hiroshima. His international perspective, administrative skills and compassionate, humanitarian views enabled Powles to build close working relationships with the Fautua, Malietoa Tanumafili II and Tupua Tamasese Mea'ole, during his decade as New Zealand's leading representative in Sāmoa.

Two months after Powles took up his role, Jim Davidson was

2   See Aikman's brief biography of Powles, 2000, 2010.

appointed by Prime Minister Fraser as Trusteeship Officer in the Sāmoan public service. The two New Zealanders, Powles and Davidson, and the Sāmoans, Malietoa Tanumafili II and Tupua Tamasese Mea'ole, worked in unison and became the key navigators of the last leg of Sāmoa's journey towards self-government.

The Legislative Assembly and the Executive Council

The Legislative Assembly and the Executive Council were the two key institutions to be established and to lead the transition to self-government. Nominations for membership of the Legislative Assembly were received from districts. Some districts nominated one candidate, who was subsequently appointed, while other districts held ballots to elect their representative. Through these processes Sāmoan participation in the political process was increased, and a group of capable, educated and experienced leaders emerged. Tofa Tomasi, Tualaulelei Mauri, Tuala Tulo, Leutele Te'o Simaile, 'Anapu Solofa, To'omata Tua, Lealaiauloto Aso, Fonoti Ioane and Tufuga Fatu were amongst the early Sāmoan members of the Legislative Assembly, and George Betham was a prominent, long-serving European member.

The Legislative Assembly dealt with broad policy matters and legislation. It was the forerunner of the parliament to be established at independence. Davidson observed that the political thinking of the Legislative Assembly was conservative, '. . . characterised by a desire for cautious advance and for maintaining a firm link with the past'.[3] The European representatives were elected by universal suffrage, but Sāmoan representation and voting rights was based on *matai* suffrage. The previous legal distinction between 'Sāmoan' and 'European' was gradually abandoned and the distinction between races reduced. A significant number of 'Europeans' had their status changed to Sāmoan, including Mrs O.F. Nelson.

The High Commissioner, Powles, proposed that an Executive Council be established to form, determine and implement the policy of the Government of Sāmoa. He suggested it be comprised of the

3   Davidson, 1976: 318. As in Chapter 4, quotes not noted belong to Davidson.

Council of State, i.e. the High Commissioner, the two Fautua, and four elected members, three Sāmoan and one European, chosen from and by the existing Legislative Assembly. Powles chaired the weekly Executive Council meetings and the elected members, including Tualaulelei, Leutele and Betham, kept the Council in touch with the wider community as policies were established and decisions were made. The Executive Council was the precursor of executive government and provided an opportunity for aspiring politicians to learn the processes and disciplines of day-to-day governance. A number of Council members would become cabinet ministers after independence.

In March 1953, following consultations in Wellington, the Prime Minister of New Zealand, the Right Honourable Sidney Holland, and the High Commissioner simultaneously issued a comprehensive statement on New Zealand's commitment to Western Sāmoa,[4] to develop:

> A strong, responsible and representative central government whose authority is accepted by the community and which is Sāmoan in outlook, personnel and in the basis of its power.
>
> A united population comprising all Sāmoan citizens regardless of race.
>
> The administrative machinery, the institutions, and the knowledge necessary for the solution of the political, social and economic problems that will come during the next generation.

The statement made the point that the developments over the five years, since the United Nations Trusteeship Council Mission had visited and the Sāmoa Amendment Act 1947 had come into effect, proved that 'New Zealand's confidence in the Sāmoan people had been amply justified'. One of the key proposals was that a constitutional convention be held by the end of 1954 to consider important constitutional matters relating to self-government.

4   Davidson, 1976: 320.

The 1954 Constitutional Convention

New Zealand adopted a relaxed approach to decolonisation and, although Powles proposed that Sāmoa follow the British parliamentary system and suggested a unicameral legislature, a House of Representatives with members elected from the traditional political districts with an executive of a Premier and Cabinet Ministers, the High Commissioner was open to alternative proposals. A working party was set up to plan, establish an agenda, and a set of procedures and organise the first Constitutional Convention.

The Constitutional Convention convened on 10 November 1954; 170 members attended the first session and the Convention ran through to 22 December. The membership was broadly representative and echoed the Fono of all Sāmoa held eight years earlier. The Fautua, Malietoa Tanumafili II and Tupua Tamasese Meaʻole, were joint chairmen, members included the members of the Legislative Assembly and Fono of Faipule, plus two other representatives from each constituency, ten additional European representatives and others representing traditional polities. This was a large and cumbersome assembly to manage. 'But . . . it enabled a broadly representative assembly to reach conclusions on major constitutional issues . . .'

There was a large range of issues considered by the Constitutional Convention. Some matters were quickly agreed to, such as the 'special relationship' with New Zealand; other matters, such as common status for Sāmoans and Europeans, were unresolved and parked for later resolution. Powles' suggestion of single legislature, presided over by a Speaker, and an executive of a Premier and Cabinet Ministers, was accepted. However, his suggestion of widening suffrage and basing constituencies on traditional districts was the subject of a long debate. A request from representatives of Tūmua and Pule districts for eleven seats to be allocated to them was not supported, and it was eventually agreed that there would be 45 seats plus two 'Individual' seats for European voters in the Apia area. The most difficult question related to the office of the Head of State as it involved Sāmoan custom and the leadership role of *tama-a-ʻāiga*.

Malietoa Tanumafili II and Tupua Tamasese Mea'ole, both *tama-a-'āiga,* vacated the chair for the discussion on the Head of State, in favour of Tualaulelei Mauri and Leutele Te'o, and withdrew from the Convention along with Fiamē Matā'afa Faumuinā Mulinu'ū and Tuimaleali'ifano Suatipatipa II, the other *tama-a-'āiga.* The debate took a week.

Maulolo, an important orator from Afega, opened the debate by supporting the proposal for the Fautua to be appointed joint Head of State and encouraged open debate. Other speakers stressed the importance of a unanimous decision. Concerns were expressed that some would be excluded from the role if the Fautua were appointed. Others suggested that a council of four be established, whilst others favoured a single Head of State. Many permutations were discussed. Throughout the debate, speakers sought national unity and attempted to put their family allegiances to one side, arguing that they had a higher duty to peace and to the nation. Finally it was recommended that Malietoa Tanumafili II and Tupua Tamasese Mea'ole be appointed joint Head of State for life, and that future vacancies should be decided by the Parliament. The resolution was carried with eight dissenting votes.

When the *tama-a-'āiga* returned for the final sitting of the Conference, Fiamē Matā'afa asked for leave to speak before the concluding speeches. After thanking the members for their work, he expressed his dissatisfaction with the decision regarding the Head of State, as it made no place for him or Tuimaleali'ifano, the other *tama-a-'āiga,* despite their rank. He stated that 'this family should refrain from taking part in future affairs of the State'. The following speakers pleaded for him not to destroy Sāmoan unity when they were so close to self-government.

Davidson later wrote: 'The success of the convention could not be measured, however, in terms only of this limited formal achievement. No less important was the fact that it had brought a large body of Sāmoans, of the most varied outlook and background, face to face with the problems of constitutional change. This had yielded a large profit in terms of political education: they, and the far larger number who had listened to the broadcasts of the convention's proceedings, were far better prepared for the difficulties that lay ahead.'

The 1954 Constitutional Convention had made a good start on an open conversation on the nature of Sāmoa's constitutional arrangements and had debated and resolved some matters. However, there was still work to do to close some of the gaps between customary and democratic governance, and to put in place a workable system of self-government.

The New Zealand Government's interim report in June 1955 accepted the majority of the proposals from the Constitutional Convention, including *matai* suffrage, noted matters requiring more work, and proposed a timetable for introducing the changes. The final report in December included a detailed plan for the transfer of executive power. A register of *matai* was established, as part of the new electoral procedures, and the Fono of Faipule was abolished. Nominations for the first general election for the Legislative Assembly closed in October 1957, and all candidates were invited to deliver an election address over the government radio station.

In 25 of the 41 Sāmoan constituencies, only one nomination was received, and these candidates were duly elected unopposed. Discussion amongst the *matai*, using traditional procedures in district *fono*, had reached a consensus of who was the best candidate in most constituencies. The remaining constituencies returned members through secret ballot. The five European members were elected through universal suffrage. Perhaps the most interesting result was the election of Fiamē Matā'afa Faumauinā Mulinu'ū II at Lotofaga. He ran in Lotofaga under his Fiamē title, rather than as Matā'afa, a *tama-a-'āiga*, having, as a relatively young man, reached the conclusion that he would have greater influence as a working politician. This decision ended the conflict that had arisen after his comments about the appointment of the joint Head of State at the Constitutional Convention, and led to greater unity.

The new Legislative Assembly met on 27 November 1957. Most members were new to politics but many were progressively minded. Luafatasaga Kalapu was chosen as Speaker and Amoa Tausilia his Deputy. Both were fluently bilingual, had been competent, senior public servants, and were familiar with governmental processes.

The Executive Council included: Tualaulelei Mauri, Tuatagaloa Leutele, To'omata Lilomaiava, Eugene Paul, Fa'alava'au Galu, Fiamē Matā'afa Faumuinā Mulinu'ū II and Frank Clemens Frederick Nelson, who were given the title and responsibilities of Minister. Eugene Paul was elected as Leader of Government Business, and the High Commissioner appointed New Zealand public servants as the Financial Secretary and the Attorney General.

With the legislature and ministers in place it was time to get on with the business of governance. The poor economic conditions of 1956–1957, and weak revenue, encouraged Eugene Paul, who held the Economic Development and Finance portfolios, to develop a practical economic plan for 1959–1961. And Powles, the High Commissioner, pushed his idea of local government, along the lines of New Zealand's, to implement rural development plans. Little progress was made, however, as there was a general view that economic development would follow, rather than precede, self-government, and there was a reluctance from the Sāmoans to take the responsibility for local governance away from the village *fono*. The focus remained on preparations for self-government.

The Working Committee on Self-Government

New Zealand had learnt from the experience of observing India's move to independence and the subsequent traumatic partition of Pakistan, and developed a clear policy of transferring responsibility to Sāmoans by stages with the understanding that the United Nations would have to agree on the termination of the Trustee Agreement. In January 1959 a Working Committee on Self-Government was established, on the recommendation of the High Commissioner, and it did not include any New Zealand public servants. The new committee was chaired by the Fautua and included the seven ministers plus seven additional members from the Legislative Assembly. Lauofo Meti was appointed Research Secretary and Jim Davidson as a constitutional adviser for the Sāmoan Government. The responsibility of preparing a draft constitution was clearly in Sāmoan hands. An early decision was made for a second constitutional convention to consider and enact the draft constitution.

The New Zealand Government had earlier appointed Professor Colin Aikman, Professor of Constitutional Law at Victoria University of Wellington, as their constitutional adviser for Sāmoa. He soon gained the confidence of the Working Committee and made a major contribution to the work of drafting the constitution. An early task was formalising Sāmoan citizenship, ahead of elections for the Legislative Assembly at the end of 1960 and the plebiscite required by the United Nations to determine the views of the Sāmoan people about achieving independence. A visiting mission from the United Nations met with the Working Committee and many others producing a constructive report on 'the question of Western Sāmoa'. The Working Committee then focused on drafting the Citizenship of Western Sāmoa Bill for the Legislative Assembly and the Sāmoa Amendment Bill for the New Zealand Parliament.

The Legislative Assembly passed the Citizenship of Western Sāmoa Bill.

The Sāmoa Amendment Act 1959 came into force on 1 October 1959. This act formalised cabinet government consisting of a prime minister, appointed on the nomination of the Legislative Assembly, and eight ministers chosen by the prime minister from members of the Assembly. The act also created a Sāmoan Public Service, headed by a Public Service Commissioner, to be responsible to the Government of Sāmoa.

With the institutions of governance now in place, the decisions on who would head them up now had to be made.

The Fautua, Malietoa Tanumafili II and Tupua Tamasese Meaʻole, who would become Joint Head of State, had taken a step back from executive government in preparation for the transition. The Legislative Assembly called for nominations for prime minister. Fiamē Matāʻafa Faumauinā Mulinuʻū II, Eugene Paul and Tualaulelei Mauri were nominated. Fiamē was the leading contender on the first ballot and achieved an absolute majority on the second ballot. His first act was to select his rivals and the outgoing ministers for his Cabinet, demonstrating his wish for unity in the transition to independence.

When he became prime minister, Fiamē was thirty-eight. Davidson described him:

> Eloquent and allusive in speech, confident but unaggressive in action, aloof but not unfriendly in manner, he had gained the respect of all and avoided close association with any group or faction. He was a leader who, like a good *matai* in his relations with his family, kept in sensitive touch with the feelings and opinions of those who had entrusted him with authority.[5]

He was also *tama-a-'āiga* through his Matā'afa title, and at a deep cultural level this gave Sāmoans confidence at this time of transition.

In April 1960, with leadership and the institutions of governance now in place, and in Sāmoan hands, Guy Powles, who for a decade had gently guided Sāmoa on its path to independence, stepped down as High Commissioner. His intelligence, talent, modesty, political skills and commitment to Sāmoan participation and partnership throughout the journey towards independence had earned him the love and respect of the people of Sāmoa and did much to build a positive relationship with New Zealand.

By July 1960 the Working Group had completed the draft constitution in preparation for a second Constitutional Convention to consider and adopt. Matters that had been 'parked' had to be resolved, including the matter of the Head of State. It was agreed that the Fautua would become Joint Head of State at independence and hold the office for life. On the death of either, the other would continue as the sole Head of State. The Legislative Assembly would then elect a single Head of State for a five-year term. A Council of Deputies would be established with members, elected after independence, to act for the Head of State in cases of absence or incapacity. Membership of the Council of Deputies would exclude '. . . a person not eligible to be elected as a Member of Parliament . . .' and who '. . . does not possess such other qualifications as the Legislative Assembly may

5   Davidson, 1976: 365.

determine from time to time by resolution . . .'[6] This carefully worded clause in the Draft Constitution provided a position for *tama-a-'āiga* not currently Head of State, and at the same time widened future eligibility. Members of the Council of Deputies were precluded from active political participation.

It was later noted that:

> At independence, the problem of what to do about *tama-a-'āiga* was finessed by appointing the paramount chiefs Malietoa Tanumafili II and Tupua Tamasese Mea'ole joint Head of State, Tuimaleali'ifano Suatipatipa to the Council of Deputies and Fiamē Matā'afa Faumuinā Mulinu'ū II Prime Minister. These appointments allowed for cultural concerns and sensitivities to be satisfied by filling the leading roles in the new democracy with customary leaders. This elegant solution would provide political stability in Sāmoa during the first critical decades after independence and build a solid foundation for the stability and continuity that has been the aim of Sāmoan governance.[7]

Other matters requiring careful consideration were the status of 'Sāmoans' and 'Europeans', and the debate between universal suffrage and *matai* suffrage. The draft constitution recognised no distinction based on 'race' but established, 'as a temporary expedient', two electoral rolls: one, based on *matai* suffrage for 'territorial' constituencies; the other, based on universal suffrage, for two 'Individual' constituencies replacing the former 'European' seats. The expectation was that over time the Sāmoan community would become fully unified.[8]

Customary land and *matai* titles are at the heart of the *fa'asāmoa* and are closely interlinked. Part IX of the Constitution deals with 'Land and Titles' and the provisions were thoroughly discussed and carefully drafted. It was agreed that: 'A *matai* title should be held in

---

6 Article 18, Clause (2).
7 Malielegaoi and Swain, 2017: 18–19.
8 Over 50 years later the Individual seats were finally abolished and after the 2016 General Election Sāmoa had a Parliament of Chiefs elected through universal suffrage.

accordance with Sāmoan custom and usage and with the law relating to Sāmoan custom and usage. 'Only Sāmoan citizens could hold *matai* titles, and Sāmoan land would be known as "customary land" and protected against alienation.' The Working Committee agreed that disputes over customary land and titles would continue to go to the Land and Titles Court for resolution.

The 1960 Constitutional Convention

Having deliberated on and reached solutions to all the difficult matters, the Working Committee had completed its task of preparing a Draft Constitution. The next step was to convene a second Constitutional Convention to reach agreement and enact The Constitution of the Independent State of Western Sāmoa.

The Convention opened on 16 August 1960. Unlike the broadly framed agenda of the 1954 Convention, the matters to consider in 1960 were detailed and specific. Members had been given copies of the Draft Constitution in July to study and it had been widely disseminated on radio and in the newspaper. The convention soon settled down to the task of considering the Draft Constitution article by article. The Fautua jointly chaired sessions with the Prime Minister as deputy chair. Each Article was read out in Sāmoan and English, a motion was moved for its adoption, and before it was opened for discussion one of the constitutional advisers would explain the article. Debate would proceed, with questions answered by the chair or advisers, until the vote was put. This procedure worked smoothly, and the positive, respectful attitude of most members, despite differences of viewpoints, steadily advanced the work of the Convention.

Matters relating to the traditional social structure of Sāmoa, land and titles, and to the Head of State, were intensely debated. A 'Note and Resolution regarding the leasing of customary land', that recommended an investigation by a select committee of the Legislative Assembly, was subject to eight hours debate and was finally agreed 92 to 70.[9] The Fautua withdrew from the debate on

9   Davidson, 1976: 392–295.

the Head of State and Fiamē Matāʻafa took the chair declaring that he had entered politics as Fiamē and had no intention of seeking the role of Head of State as a Matāʻafa and a *tama-a-ʻāiga,* saying that 'I am one of the servants of the people'. Tuimalealiʻifano Suatipatipa, the remaining *tama-a-ʻāiga,* subsequently withdrew from the debate. The arguments that had exercised the Working Group were revisited in the Constitutional Convention, amendments were moved, debated and defeated, and finally, after a fortnight of deliberating, the Articles relating to the Head of State were passed without change. Davidson would later write that the Constitutional Convention '. . . had been able to discuss most exhaustively the most difficult problem in Sāmoan politics and to endorse, at the end with unanimity, a full solution to it.'

A motion on establishing special representation for Tūmua and Pule in the Legislative Assembly led to a late sitting on 10 October but was ultimately defeated.[10] Pressure was on to finalise the Constitution and the Convention sat after midnight for several days. On 28 October the Constitutional Convention held its final meeting and agreed to adopt and enact the Constitution of the Independent State of Western Sāmoa.

The final act of the Convention was to pass a resolution regarding the future international status and external relations of Western Sāmoa, including seeking the termination of the Trusteeship Agreement from the United Nations and formalising a Treaty of Friendship between the two sovereign states of Western Sāmoa and New Zealand, to be signed after Independence Day.

Towards Independence

In December 1960, Fiamē Matāʻafa Faumauinā Mulinuʻū II joined the New Zealand Delegation to the United Nations General Assembly in New York. Frank Corner, Secretary for Foreign Affairs, told the General Assembly that New Zealand was fully committed

10 See Soʻo, 2008: 52–57 for more detail on the Tūmua and Pule debate at the Constitutional Convention.

FONO

to Western Sāmoa obtaining independence on 1 January 1962. The Prime Minister spoke in Sāmoan. A key part of his speech, translated here into English, read:

> The Sāmoan people have never wavered in their desire for independence. In earlier years – under the Germans, and then under New Zealand – the Sāmoan will to be free led to conflict and disagreement. In more recent years, Sāmoan aspirations have been fully accepted by the New Zealand Government. But, although our relations with New Zealand are – and are likely to remain – close and friendly, we believe that the time has come for us to obtain the status of an independent nation.

The United Nations passed a vote for a plebiscite to be held in Western Sāmoa on May 1961. Two questions would be asked:

> Do you agree with the constitution adopted by the Constitutional Convention on 28 October 1960?

> Do you agree that on January 1962 Western Sāmoa should become an independent state on the basis of that constitution?

In February 1961 a general election was held for the Legislative Assembly that would sit through independence. When it met, Fiamē Matā'afa Faumauinā Mulinu'ū II was elected as prime minister unopposed. He chose established leaders for his cabinet, including the former ministers, who were re-elected, and added: George Betham, Tufuga Fatu and Asiata Lagolago to replace the defeated Taualaulelei and the retiring Eugene Paul and Luamanuvae Eti.

The plebiscite was held on 9 May 1961: 83% voted 'yes' for the first question and 79 per cent for the second.[11] Fiamē Matā'afa's second visit to the United Nations in October 1961 formalised the termination of the Trusteeship Agreement. With the final hurdle

11 See Davidson, 1976: 406–7 for a discussion on the 'no' vote by a minority who were concerned about specific issues rather than the general proposition of independence.

cleared, Sāmoans could now concentrate on the final steps on the path to independence.

Church bells rang out throughout Sāmoa at midnight on 31 December 1961. On the morning of 1 January 1962 the New Zealand flag was lowered for the last time and the Sāmoan flag was raised to fly alone. The contest for the indigenous governance of Sāmoa had ended; the struggle amongst Sāmoans for political power had just begun.

Chapter 6

Indigenous Governance

Sāmoa's Parliament of Chiefs, the unique village-based form of governance developed over three millennia and centred on a fono of matai, was challenged by European powers during the 19th century and, after a long struggle, Germany won control. However, Sāmoans did not cede sovereignty. From 1914 New Zealand governed Sāmoa under international mandates until political independence was achieved in 1962. Sāmoa established a constitution that set out a new form of indigenous governance blending aspects of the faʻasāmoa and the faʻamatai within a democratic parliamentary framework. Over the following six decades successive political leaders have contested for the governance of Sāmoa. Three decades of stable governance were upset following stiff competition in the 2021 General Election.

Political Leadership in Sāmoa

Sāmoa's governance by village *fono* led by *matai* stood the test of time for millennia until it was disrupted by European powers that attempted to replace *fono* and control the governance of Sāmoa by promoting and sponsoring their favoured *matai* as the 'King' of Sāmoa. For a century local political leaders, inspired by Lauaki Namalauʻulu Mamoe, contested governance by European powers and finally re-established indigenous governance at independence.

During the period leading up to and immediately following independence, Sāmoans called on traditional political leaders, principally holders of paramount titles and *tama-a-ʻāiga*, the elite, to fill key political leadership positions. The requirement for candidates seeking political office to have a *matai* title, and demonstrate *monotaga* through serving their village community, has led to a parliament that was deeply grounded in the local processes of *fa'amatai* and *fa'asāmoa*. Slowly, new leaders emerged, including those who had gained wider experience running a business or working in government administration, as well as being a village *matai*. Few of these leaders had formal education beyond secondary school but they were familiar with the *fa'amatai* and *fa'asāmoa* and understood the social and economic needs of their communities. They expanded the pool of political candidates.

The next generation of political leaders included those who had won scholarships to attend secondary school in New Zealand and some who went on to complete university degrees. These leaders introduced new political ideas and a tension grew between the 'new school', favouring increased democratic participation and the greater participation of women in politics based on Western values, and the 'old school' of traditional elite leaders who prioritised Sāmoan values.

Political leaders have more recently emerged who are able to blend their working knowledge and experience of the *fa'amatai* and *fa'asāmoa* with a university education, international work experience and knowledge of the principles and practice of democratic good governance. Today's Parliament includes MPs with a wide variety of backgrounds, but all leaders are *matai* who have knowledge and experience of leadership in their village community providing localised wisdom that can be applied to political leadership at the national level. Adam Smith's argument that the 'dead hand' of tradition[1] holds back progress does not apply in Sāmoa. Cultural values and practices are recognised as a great strength and are the living heartbeat of Sāmoan political leaders as they face the challenges of governance in the 21st century.

---

1   In *The Theory of Moral Sentiments*, 1759, Adam Smith used the economic concept of an 'invisible hand' to describe the social benefits and public good brought about by individuals acting in their own self-interests, in opposition to the 'dead hand' of tradition holding back progress.

Premiers since Independence[2]

There has been an evolution of the style, substance and sophistication of political leadership of Sāmoa since independence. The first Prime Minister of the Independent State of Western Sāmoa, Fiamē Matāʻafa Faumuinā Mulinuʻū II,[3] was elected by the Legislative Assembly in 1959 and again in 1961 in preparation for independence in 1962. He was elected prime minister unopposed after the 1964 and 1967 general elections. Fiamē's prestigious *matai* titles, his status as *tama-a-ʻāiga* and his patrician leadership style, based on traditional Sāmoan concepts and cultural values, contributed to his lengthy leadership during the early stages of Sāmoa's political development.

Under Fiamē's leadership, consensus politics was the order of the day. The Prime Minister chose his eight cabinet ministers. As well as his political supporters, he also chose some of his political opponents as cabinet ministers and channelled their energies into their ministerial portfolios. There was no formal opposition party; those who were not ministers became the 'opposition'. This was the consensus politics of personality and persuasion, very much like traditional village governance. In a small country that was trying to find its own way in the first years of independence, and where everyone knew each other's strengths, weaknesses and family connections, these arrangements worked for a while, but were not sustainable in the long term.

The development of political parties would wait until the 1980s. In the meantime, Fiamē's leadership was unchallenged. However, after three three-year terms as prime minister, his leadership was contested, and there was a change of premier.

Tupua Tamasese Lealofi IV was elected prime minister after the 1970 general election in a close contest with Fiamē Matāʻafa and his

---

2   The material in this section is largely based on the Prologue of *Pālemia*, 2017: 17–23.

3   As discussed in Chapter 5, Fiamē Matāʻafa Faumuinā Mulinuʻu II chose to pursue a career as a 'working politician' using his Fiamē title rather than seek candidacy for Head of State or Member of the Council of Deputies as a tama-a-ʻāiga under his Matāʻafa title.

cousin the young Tupuola Tufuga Taisi Efi.[4] Tupua Tamasese Lealofi
IV had succeeded to the paramount Tupua title after the death of the
joint Head of State, Tupua Tamasese Meaʻole,[5] and continued the
leadership of Parliament by those with *tama-a-ʻāiga* lineage. Younger
political leaders, often university-educated overseas and committed
to modernisation, were starting to emerge, challenging the old guard
of village-trained, customary leaders, and questioning the view that
leadership was the prerogative of *tama-a-ʻāiga*. However, change was
gradual.

Fiamē was returned as prime minister after the 1973 general
election and held the role until his sudden death on 20 May 1975.
The Head of State, Malietoa Tanumafili II, subsequently reappointed
Tupua Tamasese Lealofi IV to replace Fiamē. This arrangement had
some critics[6] but held until the 1976 general election, due to deep
respect for *tama-a-ʻāiga* and the office of the Head of State.

Tupuola Tufuga Taisi Efi became prime minister in 1976 in a
contest against his cousin, the sitting premier Tupua Tamasese Lealofi
IV, and retained the role with a reduced majority after the 1979
general election. He was a progressive politician with a liberalising
agenda and the first non-*tama-a-ʻāiga* titleholder to become prime
minister. (Later, he would accede to the paramount title Tupua and
become a *tama-a-ʻāiga* title holder.) In his rush to wrest the prime
minister's position from Tupua Tamasese Lealofi IV, Tupuola Efi
unwittingly set the precedent for future non-*tama-a-ʻāiga* titleholders
to take over the premiership. The gentlemanly, behind-the-scenes,
consensus politics of the post-independence period was ending, as the
contest for governance was now played out in the open. Power politics
had started and turbulent times were on the horizon.

Vaʻai Kolone had contested the leadership with Tupuola Efi in 1979

4   Later known as Tui Ātua Tupua Tamasese.
5   Tupua Tamasese Meaʻole was the brother of Tupua Tamasese Lealofi IV and
     father of Tupuola Tufuga Taisi Efi.
6   Extra-constitutional appointments of a prime minister by the Head of State
     occurred on three occasions and caused considerable political tension and
     anxiety until constitutional amendments clarified the role of the Head of
     State, and Parliamentary Standing Orders established that the prime minister
     was to be the party leader commanding a majority in the House.

and was defeated by one vote, the vote of his own brother Lesatele Rapi Vaai, who was rewarded with a ministerial position in Tupuola Efi's Cabinet. Kolone was amongst the founders of the Human Rights Protection Party, together with Tofilau 'Eti Alesana[7], other former and existing Members of Parliament, and senior public servants who had been dismissed by Tupuola's government through commissions of inquiry. The alleged violation of the human rights of the public servants dismissed by Tupuola's government, and the high-handed way the young prime minister had used his public office, were the catalysts that led to the formation of the first political party in Sāmoa and also the reason for its name: the Human Rights Protection Party (HRPP).

Va'ai Kolone, a respected senior *matai* and successful businessman from Savai'i, was elected leader of the HRPP, and Tofilau 'Eti Alesana, also from Savai'i, was elected his deputy. Party politics was emerging.

In the early 1980s Sāmoa was facing major crises, both economic and constitutional. Rising prices of imported goods and declining agricultural productivity and commodity prices led to inflation running at around 38 per cent. Sāmoa was financially insolvent. A bitter Public Service Association strike dragged on for three months and left the country divided.

Eventually, public servants returned to work following a court order overturning a decision by the government to dismiss all public servants who were on strike. Ironically, the gains in salary secured by public servants came from a committee set up by the government but chaired by opposition deputy leader Tofilau 'Eti Alesana. Government ministers had run out of ideas and the HRPP politicians provided the answers. The strike was over but the residue of bitterness that the strike had generated lasted for some years and led to a change of government. Discontent over Tupuola Tufuga Taisi Efi's handling of the disruptive Public Service Association strike added impetus to a challenge of his leadership and changes to the way politics was transacted in Sāmoa.

---

7   A member of the pre-independence Legislative Assembly, formerly known as Luamanuvae 'Eti.

In the April 1982 general election, Va'ai Kolone narrowly defeated Tupuola Efi. His prime ministership was, however, short lived. An election petition in September 1982 was upheld in the Supreme Court and Va'ai Kolone's Government was removed from office. Less than 24 hours after the court ruling was made, the Head of State reappointed the recently defeated Tupuola Efi prime minister and asked him to form a government. But it also proved to be short-lived.

An electoral petition that voided the result of the Salega constituency led to a by-election that returned a HRPP Member of Parliament, upsetting the delicate balance of power in the Parliament. Another by-election on the second Saturday of October 1982 resulted in the election of another HRPP Member. The balance of power had shifted. On 21 December the government's Budget was rejected by a vote of 23 to 21, ending Tupuola's three-month third term as prime minister and opening the way for Tofilau 'Eti Alesana, now leader of the HRPP, to be elected premier on 30 December 1982. In one turbulent year Sāmoa had had four prime ministers.

Prime Minister Tofilau reappointed all of Va'ai's former cabinet ministers to his new Cabinet and added Tuila'epa Sa'ilele Malielegaoi, an independent Member of Parliament who had recently joined the HRPP, and gave him the task of restructuring the economy as Minister of Finance and Economic Development.

The HRPP won a landslide victory in the 1985 general election, gaining a two-thirds majority, but Tofilau's hold on the premiership was not secure. Va'ai Kolone, returned to Parliament through a by-election, made unsuccessful moves to get the top job back. Some HRPP members, who were unhappy that they had not been appointed to Tofilau's Cabinet, formed a breakaway faction under Va'ai Kolone's leadership and joined Tupuola's opposition party. They planned to introduce a no-confidence motion to defeat the government's Budget when Parliament was due to meet in June.

A filibuster stalled the inevitable. Finally, in December 1985, Tofilau's term ended when his 1986 Budget was defeated and he subsequently resigned. The Head of State did not take Tofilau's advice to dissolve Parliament and call new elections. Instead, he asked Va'ai Kolone to lead a coalition government for the remainder of the parliamentary term.

The 1988 general election pitted a Vaʻai Kolone-led coalition against the HRPP led by Tofilau. It was a close-run thing, with political manoeuvres from all parties and defections from both sides. Tofilau had the numbers and set about forming a government. The defeated coalition united under Tupua Tamasese who had established the Sāmoa National Development Party (SNDP), with Vaʻai as his deputy leader. Sāmoa now had two political parties, one in government, the other in opposition. Party politics had truly arrived. Ironically, Sāmoa entered into a period of greater political stability that was to last for nearly four decades.

Tofilau ʻEti Alesana introduced a legally binding pledge of allegiance for prospective HRPP Members of Parliament to strengthen and consolidate the party and avoid the divisions and defections that had split past administrations. Parliamentary under-secretary and committee chair positions were established to reward loyal government MPs, feed the ambitions of new MPs and strengthen the government caucus. Four other developments – accelerating the improvement to roads, extending electricity coverage throughout the country, protecting forestry resources through a ban on the export of logs and a national referendum on universal suffrage – consolidated support for the HRPP and led to victory in the 1991 general election.

The 27 seats won by the HRPP in 1991 were supplemented by the addition of independent Members of Parliament and defectors from the SNDP. Tofilau ʻEti Alesana won the prime ministership with 31 seats, which he later strengthened to a two-thirds majority with the support of MPs crossing the floor, enabling the passing of two bills to amend the Constitution and a law change. The first amendment added two more parliamentary seats, increasing the number to 49. The second amendment increased Cabinet posts from eight to twelve ministers.[8] The law change increased the parliamentary term from three to five years. The HRPP party apparatus was further strengthened by the election of a deputy party leader, Tuilaʻepa Saʻilele Malielegaoi, then

8   With twelve ministers and twelve under-secretaries, plus the prime minister, the government had 25 votes and a majority in the 49-member Parliament.

Minister of Finance and Deputy Prime Minister.

Tofilau 'Eti Alesana had led Sāmoa through a turbulent period and then set about putting in place reforms that would lead to a long period of political stability under stable HRPP leadership. He convincingly won the 1996 general election and continued to consolidate his legacy until his health failed in office in 1998, shortly before his death.

On 23 November 1998 Tuila'epa Sa'ilele Malielegaoi was elected Prime Minister of Sāmoa. Tuila'epa subsequently won the 2001, 2006, 2011 and 2016 general elections, to become Sāmoa's longest-serving prime minister.[9] Following the 2016 general election the HRPP government held 47 of the 50 seats in the House of Representatives, leading to criticism of Sāmoa becoming a 'one party state'.[10] In 2021, after 22 years in power, Tuila'epa sought a fifth term as Prime Minister.

The 2021 General Election – Contesting for Governance

The results of the 2021 General Election surprised many and demonstrated that the contest for political power and governance was still alive and well in Sāmoa. In 2020 a new political party, Fa'atuatua i le Atua Sāmoa ua Tasi (FAST), had been established by Laauli Schmidt, a disaffected former HRPP Minister. The FAST Party slowly built support as campaigning for the 2021 General Election started. HRPP appeared to be cruising to another win until September 2020, when Fiamē Naomi Matā'afa dramatically resigned her position as Deputy Prime Minister and her ministerial portfolios to stand as an Independent. Then, a month before the General Election, Fiamē accepted an offer of leadership of the FAST Party. It appeared that she had become disenchanted with Tuila'epa's leadership, made the calculation that Prime Minister Tuila'epa would not step down as HRPP leader in her favour, and determined that this election would be her best chance to achieve her ambition to become Prime Minister.

9 The details of Tuila'epa's premiership can be found in his memoir, *Pālemia*, 2017.

10 See *Pālemia*, 2017: 222–226.

Furthermore, Fiamē joined Opposition MPs to vote against three constitutional ammendments enacted by the HRPP Government. (See Appendix 2.)

The FAST Party vigorously campaigned for change through social media, raised money from Sāmoans overseas to fund their campaign, and promoted Fiamē as Sāmoa's first 'woman' Prime Minister. FAST targeted unpopular HRPP Government measures, including supporting the EFKS Church Ministers' refusal to pay income tax, and challenged Tuila'epa's constitutional ammendments.[11] The extensive use of Facebook and other social media was new to Sāmoan politics and became a feature of the FAST campaign. The HRPP Government was characterised by FAST as 'corrupt' and a wide range of unsubstantiated allegations were made against the Prime Minister.

Change was in the air; the contest was on. HRPP, after nearly three decades of governance and with a large parliamentary majority, took a measured approach, campaiging on its record of stable government and Tuila'epa's experienced leadership. However, it appeared that HRPP was unprepared to combat the allegations spread through social media, and had miscalculated the electorate's thirst for change. Voters were also grumpy from the stress of many months of restrictions under a State of Emergency due to the COVID-19 global pandemic. Futhermore, the HRPP strategy of running more than one candidate in a number of electorates resulted in FAST 'splitting' the HRPP vote.[12]

HRPP won the popular vote[13] in the 9 April 2021 General Election. However, the FAST Party won 24 plus 1[14] seats, equalling

11 Ironically, Fiamē Naomi Matā'afa and Laauli Leuatea Schmidt had been members of HRPP when these policies were established.
12 The overwhelming success of HRPP in the 2016 election led to many candidates seeking to run for HRPP. Sitting MPs were designated 'official' HRPP candidates, others, who thought they had a chance, were allowed by the Party to run as 'Independent HRPP' candidates. This subsequently split the HRPP vote, allowing FAST candidates to 'come up the middle', in spite of the total HRPP vote exceeding the FAST vote in a number of electorates.
13 HRPP won 55.04% of the votes, FAST 36.8%.
14 When Fiamē Matā'afa left HRPP she became an independent MP, later she was offered the leadership and joined the FAST Party.

the HRPP's 25 seats. One further independent MP was elected. The newly elected independent MP, Tuala Iosefo Ponifasio, negotiated a deal with Fiamē[15] and joined FAST, giving it a 26–25 lead. Then, the Electoral Commissioner invoked a constitutional mandate requiring a minimum of 10% female representation[16] and HRPP gained a further seat through the election of Aliʻimalemanu Alofa Tuʻuau, the next highest-polling woman candidate after five women had won constituency seats. This resulted in a 26–26 draw and an electoral impasse.

FAST quickly lodged a series of legal challenges with the courts and some defeated HRPP MPs lodged electoral petitions. The news media declared that Sāmoa was facing a 'constitutional crisis'.

On 4 May 2021, in an attempt to resolve the electoral impasse, the Head of State, Tuimalealiʻifano Vaʻaletoa Sualauvi II, met with the leaders of the two major political parties and called for fresh elections to be held on 21 May. Tuimalealiifano claimed that no party could command a majority, noted public disquiet and division, and expressed concerns about the impartiality of the court and its independence. In an address to the nation on television and radio, Tuimalealiifano said: 'Political leaders and supporters on both sides have laid serious accusations against the impartiality of the court, lessening the appearance of that arm to discharge its constitutional and common law functions to interpret and apply our laws.' Furthermore . . . 'The political discourse has done little to assist these matters.'[17]

By proposing fresh elections the Head of State was seeking to have the democratic will of the people, rather than court rulings, determine the outcome of the election. Caretaker Prime Minister Tuilaʻepa agreed with the Head of State's proposal but FAST Party Leader Fiamē Naomi Matāʻafa said that she was taken aback by the proposal and declared that she did not consider the Head of State had

---

15 Tuala drove a hard bargain. He was reported to have offered to join HRPP on the condition that Tuilaʻepa would stand down as Prime Minister, an offer that was flatly refused. Later, it became clear that the price for Tuala's membership of FAST was the deputy prime minister's role.

16 See Note on Women's Representation in Appendix 2.

17 Statement from the Head of State reported in *Sāmoa Observer*, 5 May 2021.

the constitutional power to call new elections.[18]

The FAST Party Leader, Fiamē Naomi Matā'afa, had raised the temperature of the political contest by directly and publicly challenging the Head of State,[19] and issued a media statement prior to the Head of State addressing the nation. She blamed the Caretaker Prime Minister for advising the Head of State to call fresh elections and for signing off the actions of the Electoral Commissioner in establishing an extra seat for a female MP. The FAST Party subsequently mounted legal challenges to the Head of State's declaration and to the election of Ali'imalemanu.

FAST taking legal action to resolve a political impasse was a turning point and led to the hardening of positions on both sides of the debate. The opportunity to have a *talanoaga,* a chiefly conversation, and to resolve the electoral impasse through *fa'amatai* and *fa'asāmoa* processes, was missed. Consensus decision-making, after lengthy discussions that aim to air the viewpoints and preserve the dignity of all participants, is the traditional norm for problem solving in Sāmoan chiefly society. Legal action, the subsequent court battles, and the wide use of social media as a political strategy to galvanise public opinion,[20] left participants' egos bruised, diminished the dignity of the Office of the Head of State, damaged citizens' faith in the democratic political process, and called into question the legitimacy of the new government. Many citizens were disappointed that the outcome of the 2021 General Election was finally determined by the rulings of the Supreme Court and the Appellate Court rather

18 Radio New Zealand, http: //www.rnz/international/pacific-news/441793/ sāmoa-head-of-state-calls-for-second-election, 4 May 2021, 10:06pm.

19 Rulings on constitutional matters by previous Heads of State had been accepted, albeit with some grumbling. The direct challenge of the Head of State was unprecedented.

20 A particularly nasty personal attack occurred when a FAST supporter started a petition to revoke Tuila'epa's honorary doctorate from Victoria University of Wellington, for acting 'undemocratically'. Fiamē Matā'afa was first of some 3,000 to sign. See: www.change.org. A supporter of Tuila'epa set up a counter-petition that quickly gained, 2,000 signatures. The University said, 'a revocation can only be considered in the rarest cases' and the petition did not progress.

than the votes of the people.[21]

On 17 May the Supreme Court issued two significant rulings. It overruled the declaration of the Head of State voiding the election, saying that he did not have the legal authority, and then the Court struck down the election of Ali'imalemanu as a Member of Parliament.[22] These rulings reinstated FAST's 26–25 seat lead. Furthermore, the Supreme Court reinstated the 9 April election result and directed the Head of State to reconvene Parliament within 45 days from April 9.

The Caretaker Prime Minister, Tuila'epa, spoke out against the inconsistency of these rulings, but was accused by the media as acting against the Constitution and was characterised by the FAST Party as a being a 'sore loser', defeated by Sāmoa's first female Prime Minister.[23] This quickly became the dominant media narrative, spread through social media by supporters of FAST in Sāmoa and overseas, and featured in the *Sāmoa Observer* newspaper.

On 24 May 2021, 45 days after the general election, Fiamē Maomi Matā'afa led the recently elected FAST MPs to the locked-down Parliament buildings at Mulinu'u and staged an *ad hoc* swearing-in ceremony in a tent on the *malae* of Parliament. The event was presided over by a former Attorney-General, Fiamē's personal lawyer

21 The 'separation of powers' between the executive, parliament and judiciary is a central principle of democratic governance. When a judiciary rules on electoral matters, bias may be alleged. The example of Bush v. Gore in the 2000 US presidential election is instructive. In that case: 'As much as Justices liked to present themselves as neutral arbiters, they were part of a political system too.' Baker and Glasser, 2020: 549.

22 A subsequent Appellate Court verdict ruled that six women should sit in Parliament as a minimum, but the determination of who they would be should wait until constituency seats were finalised.

23 Tuila'epa later explained: 'I am not a sore loser – and I did not engage in dirty politics. A responsible leader must always try to seek either a legal solution or a solution based on our own cultural traditions and principles of forgiveness. I tried all these. The judiciary was a disappointment . . . I was also mindful of the 60% that voted HRPP and the confidence vested in our Party leadership. To walk away knowing the numerous irregularities unfolding before our eyes, and just leaving Government with our eyes closed and without a word spoken . . . is highly irresponsible. Our God-given conscience would never allow it.' Pers. Comm.

Taulapapa Brenda Heather-Latu, with the Former Head of State, Tui Atua Tupua Tamasese Efi, in attendance to lend an air of legitimacy. Fiamē Maomi Matā'afa was declared 'Prime Minister'.

The Caretaker Prime Minister did not recognise the legality of the ceremony and Tuila'epa said it was 'treason', 'a bloodless coup', and 'a dangerous attempt by the FAST Party to seize power'.[24] The Attorney-General, Savalenoa Mareva Betham-Savalenoa, declared the swearing-in ceremony 'unconstitutional', warning that all people involved in the proceedings would be subject to civil and criminal prosecution. Savalenoa noted that neither the Head of State or a Member of the Council of Deputies, who have the authority to swear in a government, were present, nor was the Chief Justice. [25,26]

The events in Sāmoa gained international attention. New Zealand Prime Minister, Jacinda Ardern, urged Sāmoa to follow the rule of law, stating: 'We hold a huge amount of trust and faith in the institutions in Sāmoa. In the Judiciary, in their democracy and of course in the outcome that the election delivered.'[27] The United Nations' Secretary-General, Antonio Guterres, was said to be 'keeping a close eye on the situation in Sāmoa' and 'called on the leaders of the Independent State of Sāmoa to find solutions to its current political crisis through dialogue and in the best interests of the people and institutions of Sāmoa'.[28]

On 29 May Fiamē Naomi Matā'afa, now 'Prime Minister-Elect', called on the Caretaker Prime Minister, Tuila'epa, to accept his defeat and step down, saying, 'I address these comments to Tuila'epa: your long legacy is an extraordinary one of great achievement and global milestones, for which this country is rightly grateful, however, the more disruptive and disrespectful you become, the more that unique legacy is diminished and tarnished, by your own words and your own

24 Tuila'epa has consistently argued that the judiciary has not maintained its independence and challenged their rulings against HRPP.
25 Reported in *Sāmoa Observer* Online, 25 May 2021.
26 Subsequently, Prime Minister Fiamē Matā'afa suspended, then dismissed, the Attorney-General. Reported in *Sāmoa Observer* Online, 3 September 2021.
27 Reported on Newshub, 24 May 2021.
28 Reported in *Sāmoa Observer* Online, 25 May 2021.

deeds.' Fiamē concluded, '. . . it is time for this charade to end.'[29]

Tuila'epa set out his views of the political situation in an address on 31 May, the eve of Sāmoa's 59th independence anniversary. He spoke to a large gathering at the HRPP Malae o Tiafau, following a peaceful march of 500 female supporters, and outlined the chronology of events. Then he said: 'It is our priority to see the next Government is lawfully formed pursuant of the Constitution of Sāmoa and it is crucial that the rule of law is respected and followed.' Tuila'epa stated: 'In our small country of only 200,000 people we are all connected through our extended family system . . .' [and] '. . . the traditional consensus process was the most appropriate way to move forward from crisis as it allowed Sāmoan cultural and religious traditions to bring harmony and peace to the resolution of challenges.'[30]

The Head of State used his Independence Day message to Sāmoa '. . . to seek and ask God's peace' and '. . . to begin its journey to healing and dignity'. He urged leaders to seek '. . . unity, reconciliation and forgiveness'.[31]

Peace and harmony were in short supply. The Catholic Archbishop, Alapati Lui Mataeliga, used his Independence Eve Mass sermon to '. . . lash out at the HRPP-led caretaker Government and its leadership over the country's constitutional crisis . . .' and the refusal of Tuila'epa to concede defeat. He '. . . warned the country is sliding into dictatorship', and quoted Lord Acton in his homily, 'power corrupts and absolute power corrupts absolutely'. The Archbishop lectured Tuila'epa: '. . . a good son will listen to his father . . .' [and] declared '. . . your time is done'.[32] Tuila'epa listened to the sermon from his front row seat at the Cathedral of Immaculate Conception.[33]

Meanwhile, the Appellate Court ruled on the matter of female representation. It concluded, 'Although we have found that 10 per cent means 6 women in Parliament it remains to be seen whether the

29 Reported in *Sāmoa Observer* Online, 29 May 2021.
30 Reported in *Sāmoa Observer* Online, 1 June 2021.
31 Reported in *Sāmoa Observer* Online, 2 June 2021.
32 The sermon was reported extensively in *Sāmoa Observer* Online, 1 June 2021.
33 A week later Archbishop Alapati Lui Mataeliga came to Tuila'epa's residence seeking forgiveness from Tuila'epa for his remarks. Personal communication.

second respondent [Ali'imalemanu Alofa Tu'uau] will be appointed as an additional member to satisfy the requirement.'[34] Consequently, the inclusion of another female MP in the Legislative Assembly could be months away after all election results, including by-elections, were finalised. This ruling reduced the HRPP numbers. The Deputy Leader of HRPP, Fonotoe Lauofo Pierre Meredith, noted that some 28 petitions and counter-petitions had been lodged with the Supreme Court and said that '. . . that no Government should be formed until all election-related legal issues had been sorted out.' He urged the judiciary to '. . . speed up the election petition process.'[35]

The Supreme Court was now under pressure to rule on a number of matters. It held hearings on the constitutionality of the swearing-in ceremony and hearings of electoral petitions and counter-petitions. The FAST Party and Fiamē Naomi Matā'afa also filed contempt of court cases against Prime Minister Tuila'epa and Attorney-General Savalenoa, alleging that the Prime Minister had 'scandalised' the Court and disobeyed court orders to convene Parliament.[36]

Hearings of the 28 petitions went on for some weeks with rulings from the Supreme Court released from late June. A number of electoral petitions and counter petitions were withdrawn or dismissed, others were upheld. Some MPs and candidates were found guilty of charges of bribery and treating. Seven court rulings went against HRPP MPs and candidates, leaving 18 HRPP Members of Parliament. Seven by-elections were triggered.

On 28 June the Supreme Court ordered Parliament to convene in seven days (by Monday 5 July) and declared the FAST swearing in ceremony 'unlawful' and void. The Court also stated that anyone found to be standing in the way of its ruling could be prosecuted for contempt of court and that the FAST Party could be automatically sworn in if its (the Court's) instructions were ignored. Tuila'epa questioned the Court's orders, saying, 'The Judiciary does not demand

34 Reported in *Sāmoa Observer* Online, 2 June 2021.
35 Reported in *Sāmoa Observer* Online, 6 June 2021.
36 Recounting all the details of the court cases and electoral petitions is unnecessary for this narrative. Interested readers and researchers can access further details through the records of Sāmoa's Department of Justice.

[Parliament to convene] – this is stipulated in the Constitution - that is solely within the powers of the Head of State.' He also insisted that Parliament could only now be 'properly constituted' after petitions and by-elections, as ruled by the Court of Appeal, and the invoking (if necessary) of a requirement that a minimum of six female MPs be present in Parliament.[37] He again questioned the independence and competence of the judiciary and HRPP lodged a complaint with the Judicial Service Commission.

At 10pm on Sunday 4 July the Head of State announced that the Legislative Assembly would sit on 2 August. In a special announcement on TV1, and in a carefully written statement, Tuimalealiifano Vaʻaletoa Sualauvi II said, 'The Supreme Court has no jurisdiction to order the convening of Parliament as I, the Head of State of the Independent State of Sāmoa, have the powers to appoint the time and place for the meeting of the Legislative Assembly.' He further noted, 'There is uncertainty as far as the number of the Legislative Assembly is concerned therefore Parliament cannot be properly convened at this time.' On reporting the Head of State's statement the *Sāmoa Observer* declared that '. . . this puts him on a collision course with the Supreme Court'.[38]

Parliament did not convene on Monday 5 July.

At 4.30pm on Friday 23 July, three Judges of the Court of Appeal[39] handed down their ruling that the FAST Party was Sāmoa's legitimate government and that Fiamē Naomi Matāʻafa was Prime Minister, backdated to 24 May 2021.[40] The Appellate Court cited the 'doctrine of necessity' in reversing the earlier Supreme Court decision that the impromptu swearing in ceremony was illegal.

New Zealand Prime Minister, Jacinda Ardern, promptly congratulated Fiamē Naomi Matāʻafa on her victory and said that she was looking forward to working with Sāmoa's new government.

---

37 Reported in *Sāmoa Observer* Online, 3 July 2021.

38 *Sāmoa Observer* Online, 5 July 2021.

39 Chief Justice Perese, Justice Tuatagaloa and Justice Tuala-Warren.

40 This ruling was an ironic echo of the Supreme Court decision of 31 December, 1898 ruling that Matāʻafa Iosefo was deemed ineligible and that Malietoa Tanumafili I was anointed to be 'King' of Sāmoa. (See Chapter 2.)

Tuila'epa Sa'ilele Malielegaoi did not concede that he had lost the election and said the Court of Appeal decision was 'unconstitutional' and 'lacked any legal basis'. However, he accepted the ruling, saying '. . . contesting the ruling would have led to anarchy'.[41,42] Later he stated: 'The time for politics is over. It is now time for nation building.'[43,44]

On Saturday 24 July the new Prime Minister met with key government officials and directed the Treasury to prepare a budget to continue the operations of government, and key initiatives from the FAST Party Manifesto, including the promise to provide each electorate with WST$1 million for grassroots district development.

The next day the Head of State addressed the nation, giving his blessing to Fiamē Naomi Matā'afa as Sāmoa's first female Prime Minister and thanking and acknowledging Tuila'epa Sa'ilele Malielegaoi for his service as the country's leader since 1998. Tuimalealiifano Va'aletoa Sualauvi II said that he was saddened by the part of the Court of Appeal's decision that stated he did not understand the powers of the office of Head of State and the powers of the courts. He defended his role in events, outlined his deep knowledge and experience as a police officer and lawyer, and his service as a *matai*, saying that the criticism was '. . . not easy to take'. He graciously concluded by calling for safety and peace, and the protection of God over Sāmoa: *'Ou te manatu 'o se āmataga lelei lea tātou te faatagaisia ai le ta'ita'iga mamana a le Atua i ta'ita'i o Sāmoa, e fa'amanuia mai i lo 'outou faiva a mālō, 'auā le lipoiina o 'upufai o le Palemene mo le paea'iga lona sefulu*

41 Radio New Zealand International, 23 July 2021.
42 Tuila'epa consistently defended his challenges to court rulings and FAST media statements. On 30 September, 2021 he wrote a detailed Response to the Joint Communication of the Office of the UN High Commissioner of Human Rights, spelling out his defence to a wide range of allegations aired in the media.
43 Pers. Comm., 17 January 2022.
44 Later, the leaders of FAST and HRPP signed a Harmony Agreement and agreed to drop further legal proceedings, as they were taking a long time to resolve and were leading to increased conflict and mounting costs. https://tpplus.co.nz/community/sāmoa-opposition-leader-tuilaepa-says-sorry/. See Appendix 4.

ma le fitu. 'Ia faimalū lo 'outou faiva.[45]

The Friday 23 July court decision finally clarified the legal status of the FAST swearing-in ceremony of 24 May, and on Monday 26 July Tuila'epa held a press conference at the HRPP Headquarters conceding defeat and welcoming the FAST Government, led by Fiamē Naomi Matā'afa, with a warning that the HRPP will be the 'strongest opposition', and '. . . will continue to do what it always has done, and that is to work hard and serve its people'. He also advised the heads of the Public Service to support the new administration and continue their hard work. While accepting defeat, Tuila'epa remained critical of the decision of the Court saying that it 'had destroyed the Constitution'.[46] In the days that followed, Tuila'epa continued to explain that he had given his blessings to the new government, to keep the peace within the country, but he could not accept the reasons behind the Court's decisions.

Fiamē Naomi Matā'afa chaired her first cabinet meeting on 27 July and announced her Deputy Prime Minister, the former Independent Tuala Tevaga Iosefo Ponifasio, and her cabinet ministers. The FAST Government got on with the business of governing. Early priorities were preparing a budget, and sorting out the Public Service.

Aiono Mose Su'a, the Chair of the Public Service Commission. had resigned the day the new government was announced. The CEO of the Ministry of Finance, Leasiosiofaasisna Oscar Malielegaoi, had completed his budget preparations when on 28 August the new Minister of Finance, Mulipola Anarosa Ale Molio'o, asked him to resign, alleging that Leasiosiofaasisina '. . . has a conflict of interest as his father Tuila'epa Sailele Mailelegaoi was Leader of the Opposition and would challenge the budget'.[47] The Attorney-General, Savalenoa Mareva Betham-Savalenoa, was next to be sacked, and the contract of Afamasaga Fa'auiga Mulitalo, the CEO of the Ministry of Women Community and Development, was not renewed. Prime Minister Fiamē Naomi Matā'afa dismissed claims that her administration is booting out top public servants, saying '. . . her party does not have a

45 http://sāmoaglobalnews.com, 25 July 2021.
46 *Sāmoa Observer* Online, 26 July 2021
47 *Loop Pacific*, 28 August 2021.

policy to sack the nation's existing top public servants'. Explaining that she did not have confidence in the Attorney-General and the Clerk of the Legislative Assembly, Tiatia Graeme Tualaulelei,[48] because they were cited in a contempt of court case due to their actions over the swearing-in ceremony.[49]

A group of 'concerned and affected public servants' raised their concerns over the 'suspension, forced resignations and termination' of CEOs in an Open Letter to the Prime Minister dated 27 August 2021. Noting that public servants have been disrespected, undermined and intimidated and that morale is declining, mental health has been affected and 'merit based recruitment has been disregarded through appointment of government preferred advisers', they asked the new government to have confidence in the professionalism of public servants 'to continue our service to Sāmoa'.[50]

Over the next few weeks Tuila'epa continued his criticism of the judiciary and urged for Parliament to be called. When Parliament was finally called to sit on Tuesday 14 September, the new Speaker of the House, Papali'i Li'o Ta'eu Masipau, refused to swear in the 18 HRPP Members-elect. He had ordered the police to set up a barricade and notices declaring Parliament buildings and the surrounding grounds out of bounds for all members of public, and to prevent the HRPP Members from attending Parliament.[51] The FAST Government, claiming that they had a quorum,[52] started the first session of Parliament with the Budget debate, but without any Opposition MPs present.

The HRPP Members, attempting to enter Parliament to be sworn in, were blocked by Police officers but peacefully retreated. Tuila'epa announced that he was 'sad and disappointed . . . [and stated that]

48 The Speaker later terminated the Clerk's contract. *Sāmoa Observer* Online, 23 September 2021.
49 *Sāmoa Observer* Online, 28 August 2021.
50 Open Letter from Affected and Concerned Public Servants to the Prime Minister, 27 August 2021.
51 Radio New Zealand International, 14 September 2021.
52 The Speaker explained that the quorum was 23 as Parliament has 44 seats with 7 seats void awaiting the outcome of by-elections. FAST held 25 seats and HRPP, 18. Radio New Zealand International, 14 September 2021.

. . . this is the darkest day in the history of democracy in this country. The events of 14 September have tarnished the reputation of Sāmoa.' HRPP then filed an application to the Supreme Court for a declaratory order against the Speaker challenging his decision not to allow the HRPP members to enter Parliament to be sworn in.[53]

Tuila'epa and his 17 MPs returned the next morning, seeking to attend Parliament and be sworn in. Again they faced a police blockade and tensions rose. Tuila'epa spoke with the police, questioning their need to guard Parliament. He said, '. . . your job is to act when there are threats, yet there are no threats. All we want is to speak to the Speaker of the House. This is our culture, we are here to talk.'[54] The Speaker would not come out, and police would not budge and ordered the HRPP Members to leave in five minutes or be arrested. They stood their ground and a dramatic confrontation appeared inevitable as the Police brought in vehicles in preparation for removing the MPs.

Unprecedented events then unfolded in the Parliament grounds. The Catholic Archbishop, Alapati Lui Mataeliga, staged an *ifoga* in front of the Parliamentary building, seeking peace and forgiveness. The Ministers of the National Council of Churches publicly prayed outside Parliament for peace and reconciliation. The Head of State and his wife arrived at Parliament, with a police escort. Tuimalealiifano Va'aletoa Sualauvi II spoke with and embraced Tuila'epa then headed into the back entrance of the parliamentary chamber to appeal to the Speaker. Shortly after, he reappeared and returned to his residence at Vailele. The Prime Minister, who had called an early adjournment of the debate, was diven to Vailele accompanied by the Speaker.

The confrontation outside Parliament ended when a police officer told Tuila'epa that the order to arrest the MPs had been cancelled.

After meeting with the Head of State at Vailele, the Prime Minister issued a statement: 'We have assured His Highness and the Council of Deputy that all is calm and to leave it to us, the chosen members of the country to deal with these things and sort out the differences between parties, under the guidance of the Constitution.'[55]

53 *Sāmoa Observer* Online, 14 September 2021.
54 *Sāmoa Observer* Online, 14 September 2021.
55 Reported in *Sāmoa Observer* Online, 15 September 2021.

On Thursday 16 September, the Supreme Court issued an interim order, stating that 'no steps will be taken in respect to the membership of the Human Rights Protection Party's unsworn elected member until it hears an urgent application filed by the party.' Later, on Thursday evening, the Supreme Court released their ruling that the Speaker has a duty to swear in the HRPP elected members.[56]

Finally, on Friday 17 September 2021, the 18 HRPP Members of Parliament were sworn in. Tuila'epa Sa'ilele Malielegaoi, now Leader of the Opposition, crossed the floor and shook hands with Prime Minister Fiamē Naomi Matā'afa, peacefully ending[57] the 2021 contest for the governance of Sāmoa.

56 See Tabangcora, 2021, for her analysis of Sāmoan court decisions and support of the judiciary.
57 Following a series of electoral petitions, seven by-elections were ordered. The FAST Party won four, HRPP two, and one was decided by the Court that determined, on the day before the by-election, the HRPP candidate was not eligible to stand, leaving the FAST Party candidate unopposed. Subsequently, two female HRPP candidates were elected MPs to meet the constitutional requirement of, 10% of women in parliament. The Speaker refused to swear in the female MPs and the HRPP sought a ruling from the Supreme Court. On 11 May 2022 the Supreme Court ordered the Speaker of the House to administer the Oath of Allegiance for three additional female MPs: Aliimalemanu Alofa Tuua, Faagasealii Sopa Feagai (HRPP) and Toomata Norah Leota (FAST), resulting in 54 seats in the Legislative Assembly: FAST 31, HRPP, 22. A by-election for Gagaaifomauga No. 2, finalised on 4 June 2022, resulted in the election of Independent candidate Fo'isala Lio Tu'u Ioane, who subsequently said that he will join the FAST Party.

Afterword

Fono – The Contest for the Governance of Sāmoa has told the story of the development of Sāmoa's unique system of governance and those who have shaped the Independent State of Sāmoa. The 2021 General Election was a hard-fought contest for governance that tested the strength of Sāmoa's constitutional arrangements and highlighted the fragile nature of the balance of power between the executive, the judiciary and the parliament. After electoral petitions were resolved, and before by-elections completed and two women were elected to fulfil the 10% quota, the final result of Sāmoa's 2021 General Election was declared.[1] Parliament was convened on 14 September 2021 and a new Prime Minister and her Government took on the task of governing Sāmoa.

The outcome of the 2021 General Election raised more questions than answers. What have we learnt about Sāmoa's constitutional arrangements and political processes from the 2021 contest for governance? Are they fit for purpose? Do there need to be changes? And what are the fates of the key contestants in the latest struggle for the governance of Sāmoa? What challenges do they face? Seeking answers, we start with the key players.

Fiamē Naomi Matā'afa

Fiamē Naomi Matā'afa became Sāmoa's first female Prime Minister in 2021, 60 years after Sāmoa gained independence. In 1962, as a

---

1   On 30 November 2021, two female HRPP MPs were elected to Parliament to fulfil the 10 per cent quota, however the Speaker refused to swear them in and subsequently the HRPP sought a declaratory order from the Supreme Court.

four-year-old she watched her father Fiamē Matāʻafa Faumuinā Mulinuʻu II become the first Prime Minister of the Independent State of Western Sāmoa. The symmetry is inescapable.

When Fiamē Matāʻafa Faumuinā Mulinuʻu II died suddenly on 20 May 1975, his daughter was studying at Victoria University in Wellington, New Zealand. His wife, Laulu Fetauimalemau Matāʻafa, secured his Lotofaga parliamentary seat for two terms and Naomi Matāʻafa, as she was then, returned to Sāmoa. She later acceded to her father's title of Fiamē and in 1985 entered parliament as the Member of Parliament for Lotofaga. Like her father, she chose to be a working politician. During her three decades in parliament Fiamē Matāʻafa held a number of ministerial portfolios. She was a longstanding Minister of Education and served more recently as Minister for Natural Resources and the Environment, and Deputy Prime Minister. Fiamē resigned her portfolios to run as an Independent for the 2021 General Election before accepting the leadership of the FAST Party.

Prime Minister Fiamē Naomi Matāʻafa now faces a number of challenges. The FAST Party was established by Laʻauli Schmidt as a vehicle to challenge the incumbent Prime Minister, Tuilaʻepa Saʻilele Malielegaoi. FAST's disparate membership was initially united only in their opposition to Tuilaʻepa and his HRPP Government. Many of the new FAST MPs, including Deputy Prime Minister Tuala Iosefo Ponifasio, have no parliamentary or governance experience. A major challenge for the new Prime Minister will be uniting her caucus, developing a coherent policy and legislative agenda, maintaining party unity, and ministerial and parliamentary discipline within her large number of new ministers, Members of Parliament and political neophytes as they face a determined and experienced Opposition.

Prime Minister Fiamē Naomi Matāʻafa faces multiple challenges at home and in the wider Pacific region including: maintaining economic sustainability in an uncertain global economy; reducing the impacts of global climate change and extreme weather events; ensuring the safety and security of people and resources; maintaining political independence in the context of heightened geopolitical activity and competition in the region, and responding to a global pandemic. Having won the premiership, do she and her government have the skills, knowledge, capacity, stamina and wisdom to govern and navigate Sāmoa through these turbulent times? The answer to that question will be determined as her leadership is tested in the months and years ahead.

Tuila'epa Sa'ilele Malielegaoi

Tuila'epa Dr Sa'ilele Malielegaoi was unhappy with the outcome of the 2021 General Election. He was convinced that the rulings of the judiciary had an undue influence on the outcome of the election and that unfair allegations against him, aired through social media, local newspapers and the subject of a report[2] by two United Nations human rights rapporteurs, damaged his reputation. Tuila'epa responded to the allegations made against him,[3] and then, accepting his defeat, set out to reorganise his HRPP MPs into a strong parliamentary opposition.

After four decades in Parliament, 22 years as Sāmoa's longest serving Prime Minister and the Pacific region's pre-eminent statesman, questions will be raised about Tuila'epa's political future. There is an old saying: 'Politics is like cricket: everyone gets bowled out.' Has Tuila'epa completed his innings? He has had a long, distinguished and successful premiership. Is it time for him to step down and pass the leadership of HRPP to a new leader? In his memoir, *Pālemia*, Tuila'epa obliquely reflected on his succession by talking about his own rise under Tofilau Eti Alesana[4]. He talked about watching, listening and learning to be a Member of Parliament, then becoming 'Minister of Everything', until it became obvious he was next in line to lead when Tofilau's health failed.

There was no obvious successor ready to take over the leadership from Tuila'epa to contest the 2021 General Election.

2   See United Nations, 2021. *Report of United Nations Human Rights Special Rapporteurs on the independence of judges and lawyers* and the Working Group on the discrimination against women and girls.
3   Seven allegations were made in The Joint Communication of the Office of the High Commissioner of the United Nations Human Rights cited above.
4   Malielegaoi and Swain, 2017: 262–263.

Fonotoe Lauofo Pierre Meredith, now the Deputy Leader of HRPP, contended with Fiamē Naomi Matāʻafa for the Deputy Prime Minister's role in 2016, but neither had the political support in 2020 to contest Tuilaʻepa's leadership. Will Fonotoe make another move, now that Fiamē has left HRPP, or are there other ambitious MPs ready to contend for the HRPP leadership? Or, perhaps a new aspirant will enter the contest? Time will tell if Tuilaʻepa Saʻilele Malielegaoi will continue to contest for the governance of Sāmoa.

Political Parties

The Human Rights Protection Party is the only political party in Sāmoa that has changed leaders a number of times, maintained its integrity as an organisation and demonstrated longevity. All other Sāmoan political parties have been the personal vehicle of their founder and then dissolved or died along with the leader. Faʻatuatua i le Atua Sāmoa ua Tasi (the FAST Party) was established by Laauli Schmidt who is now the party president. He stepped aside as Party Leader in favour of Fiamē Naomi Matāʻafa. Will he continue to be happy to play second fiddle?

The FAST Party made many promises during the 2021 election campaign and will need to deliver on those promises. Like all political parties, FAST will learn that it easier to promise than to deliver. Issues such as overturning the taxation of church ministers, giving voting rights to overseas-based Sāmoan citizens, and the repeal of recent constitutional amendments, had populist appeal during the campaign but may prove more difficult to implement when it comes to securing political support to enact new legislation. Will the FAST Party be able to develop an organisation that remains united and survive beyond one electoral cycle, or will it splinter under the pressures of government? Will the HRPP be able to bounce back from defeat, rejuvenate itself in opposition and have fresh leadership to contest the next election?

The Head of State

In May 2021, when a political impasse was reached, the Head of State, Tuimaleali'ifano Va'aletoa Sualauvi II, attempted to establsh a *talanoaga* between Tuila'epa and Fiamē, calling for fresh elections. Fiamē responded by questioning the Head of State's constitutional authority and sought a court ruling against the Head of State. Later, she also challenged him on his declaration voiding the election. On two previous occasions[5] a Head of State has intervened to resolve a political crisis, and while there was some private disquiet at the time there was no public challenge to the interventions. The direct questioning of the authority of the Head of State was therefore unique and the Supreme Court's subsequent rulings brought into sharp relief the fragility of the balance of powers between the executive, judiciary and Parliament. Will the judicial rulings undermine the role of the Head of State in the long term?

The role of the Head of State was the matter discussed most exhaustively in both Constitutional Conventions leading up to Independence. Part of those discussions was about the place of *tama-a-'āiga* in Sāmoa's constitutional arrangements. To date, each Head of State has been a holder of a *tama-a-'āiga* title and stood above politics. This has served to enhance the dignity of the office. There must be questions about constitutional roles and responsibilities that need to be clarified, now that the authority of the Head of State has been directly challenged by an elected official, and the Supreme Court has overruled the declaration of the Head of State voiding the election. It is notable that a former Head of State involved himself in politics by attending the swearing-in ceremony staged in a tent outside of Parliament Buildings by the FAST Party. The Supreme Court later declared the swearing-in illegal but the damage to the dignity of the office of the Head of State was already evident. What now is the future of the Office of the Head of State, and the place of *tama-a-'āiga,* in Sāmoa's constitutional arrangements?

---

5   See above, Chapter 6, Footnote 6.

The Judiciary

On 17 May 2021, when the two leading political parties were tied 26–26 and a political impasse was in play, the Supreme Court overruled the declaration of the Head of State voiding the election and struck down the election of Ali'imalemanu as a Member of Parliament, opening the way for Fiamē Naomi Matā'afa, Leader of the FAST Party, to form a government. The outcome of Sāmoa's 2021 General Election was decided by court rulings (rather than citizens' votes). This matter is at the core of Tuila'epa's accusations of judicial interference and bias and his questioning of the independence of some members of the judiciary.

Sāmoa is a small country. People are related and the *fa'asāmoa* operates on the basis of relationships. Consequently, it is difficult for any person to be truly independent, and judges often find themselves in situations where they must recuse themselves from hearing cases involving people they know well or are related to. The constitutional amendments enacted by the HRPP Government, in close consultation with the Chief Justice and the President of the Land and Titles Court, related primarily to the reorganisation of the judiciary and to land and titles. Members of the judiciary were rightly very interested in the content of the bills as they progressed through the parliamentary processes of drafting, consultation and enactment. Some members of the judiciary publicly criticised the constitutional amendments before the bills were enacted.[6] Once laws are enacted by Parliament it is the role of the judiciary to interpret and make rulings on those laws.

An independent judiciary is an important foundation for democratic governance. Any judicial bias can undermine those foundations. There is a convention that politicians should not publicly criticise the judiciary. When Tuila'epa criticised the judiciary he was soundly attacked from all quarters, including in the *Report of United Nations Human Rights Special Rapporteurs on the independence of*

6 The *Sāmoa Observer* published a confidential letter, dated 6 April 2020, to the Executive Director of the Sāmoa Law Reform Commission, signed by a number of District Court and Supreme Court Judges, supporting the Sāmoa Law Society campaign against the legislation.

judges and lawyers. This raises the question: are unelected members of the judiciary above criticism from elected politicians?

Clearly established and well-maintained boundaries between the judiciary, the executive and parliament are important for effective democratic governance. It is helpful if citizens are well informed and understand the different roles and responsibilities of the three pillars of governance. The words of Lord Jonathan Sumption, said in his 2019 Reith Lecture, are helpful in this regard:

> It is the proper function of the Courts to stop governments exceeding or abusing their legal powers. But allowing judges to circumvent parliamentary legislation or review the merits of policy decisions for which ministers are answerable to parliament, raises quite different issues. It confers vast discretionary powers on a body of people who are not constitutionally accountable to anyone for what they do. It also undermines the single biggest advantage of the political process, which is to accommodate the divergent interests and opinions of citizens.[7]

Three thousand years ago small groups of people ventured into the blue Pacific Ocean. They discovered islands rich in natural resources, settled in to self-governing village communities, and later spread throughout the region. The people of the Sāmoan islands developed a rich and complex culture and a system of governance through *Fono*, which was disrupted by European explorers, traders, missionaries, sailors, and politicians with their imperial ambitions in the 19th century. Sāmoan resistance, inspired by Lauaki Namulauʻulu Mamoe and others, finally led to political independence and self-governance in 1962. Sixty years on, six men and one woman have governed Sāmoa as Prime Minister. The contest for governance amongst Sāmoans has been and continues to be robust. Sāmoans have been able to resolve their differences, without civil conflict or outside intervention, maintaining their sovereignty and independence, and have developed a dynamic, contested and peaceful Pacific democracy.

7   See Sumption, J., 2019, Reith Lecture.

Appendix 1

Tama-a-'āiga Lineages

Malietoa, Matā'afa, Tupua and Tuimaleali'ifano are recognised as the *pāpā*, the four paramount titles, of Sāmoa. Malietoa Vai'inupō, the last to hold all four *pāpā*, was acknowledged as the *Tafa'ifā*, '. . . the closest political framework Sāmoa had to that of a central government as it is understood in the modern sense.'[1] During the 19th century the great powers (Germany, The United States, Great Britain and, to a lesser extent, France), in their attempts to gain political control of Sāmoa, selected and promoted various holders of paramount titles to become 'King' of Sāmoa. The following lists of *Tama-a-'āiga* lineages[2], from the 19th century to the present day, will assist readers to keep a track of this complex and contested narrative. Photographs (after page 100) put faces to the names of some of the key players.

Malietoa

Malietoa Ti'alematagi

Malietoa Fitisemanu (d. 1800)

Malietoa Vai'inupō (d. 1841)

Malietoa Taimalelagi Gatuitasina (d. 1858)

Malietoa Mōlī (d. 1858 or 1860)

(Malietoa Talavou (d. 1880) installed by a rival faction to M. Mōlī)

Malietoa Laupepa (d. 1898)

Malietoa Tanumafili I (d. 1939)

Malietoa Tanumafili II (d. 2007)

Malietoa Faamausili Mōlī (current title-holder)

1 So'o, 2008: 10.
2 Gathered from several sources including: Davidson, 1967; Gilson, 1970; So'o, 2008 and Tuimaleali'ifano, 2006.

Matā'afa

Fa'asuamale'aui (d. 1785)

Silupevailei (d. 1790)

Matā'afa Filifilisounu'u (d. 1829)

Matā'afa Tafagamanu (d.1863)

Matā'afa Iosefo (d. 1912)

Matā'afa Iose (d. 1915)

Matā'afa Salanoa Muliufi (d. 1936)

Matā'afa Faumuinā Fiame Mulinu'u I (d. 1948)

Matā'afa Faumuinā Fiame Mulinu'u II (d. 1975)

Matā'afa Pu'ela Fa'asuamaleaui Patu (d. 1996)

Matā'afa Lui Iosefa Tupuola (d. 2014)

The Matā'afa title is currently vacant (2022)

Tupua

Tupua Tamasese Titimaea (d.1891)

Tupua Tamasese Lealofi I (d. 1915)

Tupua Tamasese Lealofi II (d. 1918)

Tupua Tamasese Lealofi III (d. 1929)

Tupua Tamasese Mea'ole (d.1963)

Tupua Tamasese Lealofi IV (d. 1983)

Tupua Tamasese Tupuola Tufuga 'Efi (current title-holder)

Tuimaleali'ifano

Tuimaleali'ifano Suatipatipa I

Tuimaleali'ifano Sualauvi I (d. 1870)

Tuimaleali'ifano Fa'aoloi'i (d. 1937)

Tuimaleali'ifano Suatipatipa II (d. 1974)

Tuimaleali'ifano Va'aletoa Sualauvi II (current title-holder)

Appendix 2

Constitutional Amendments

The rise of the FAST Party was, in part, a result of controversy over three constitutional amendments passed into law by a 46–4 majority vote[1] in December 2020. Fiamē Naomi Matā'afa cited her unease with these constitutional amendments as a reason for her split from HRPP, in which she had served for three decades, and subsequently taking up the leadership of the FAST Party.

Constitutional amendments have in the main been uncontroversial, and the Constitution of the Independent State of Sāmoa has stood the test of time, confirming and endorsing the decisions the founding fathers made during the pre-independence Constitutional Conventions. Over the six decades since independence, several constitutional amendments and law changes have been enacted with the aim of strengthening Sāmoa's governance, and meeting changing circumstances, as well as addressing emerging and evolving social and political considerations, such as the changing role of women. Most of the constitutional amendments have been uncontroversial; however, some have led to significant public debate, demonstrating that Sāmoans are committed to and engaged in the process of debating, shaping and managing the governance of Sāmoa.

Tofilau 'Eti Alesana introduced three significant changes in 1991 and a further change to the constitution in 1997. The introduction of universal suffrage in 1991 was designed to broaden political participation by giving the vote to more women and to younger people. The addition of two further parliamentary seats in 1991 was in response to population growth. Two additional Cabinet ministerial positions were added in 1991, reflecting the increasing complexity of governance and the need to spread the administrative load.

1 Exceeding the constitutional requirement for a two-thirds majority.

Changing the nation's name from *Western Sāmoa* to *Sāmoa*, or more formally *The Independent State of Sāmoa*, through the Constitutional Amendment Act (No. 2) 1997 was the last of Tofilau's constitutional amendments and can be seen as an assertion of indigenous sovereignty, removing one of the last vestiges of imperial naming following the partition of Sāmoa a century earlier.

In 2017 Prime Minister Tuila'epa Sa'ilele Malielegaoi reflected on the reasoning behind several constitutional amendments he has implemented:

We have been gradually working towards creating a Parliament of Chiefs. Firstly, in 2006–11, we brought about the requirement that everybody must be a *matai*. We had two Individual Voters' seats that were established at independence for non-*matai*. In the election of 2011 Joe Keil resigned. He did not want to come back because he refused to take on a *matai* title. But, although complete, the fact remained that the two Individual Voters' seats still existed in the Constitution. So we had to go further and formally eliminate those two seats, and we replaced them with two 'Urban' seats. To eliminate these two seats required an amendment to the Constitution. That's what we did in November 2015.

That is why in one of my public speeches I mentioned that this new Parliament is historical for a number of reasons. Firstly, the Parliament of Sāmoa is now comprised only of Sāmoan *matai*. That reflects the true nature of a Sāmoa *fono* where only *matai* exchange ideas and make decisions on the future of the village, and now on the future of this country. Secondly, we have achieved what we aimed to do with changes to the Constitution, to ensure that more women come into Parliament. Now we have the greatest number of women ever, including two ministers. In achieving that, we had to activate the new law and increase the number of MPs. For the first time we have 50 MPs. Four women were elected to seats and the other came in as the highest polling woman to make up the required minimum of 10% female MPs.[2]

2 See *Pālemia*, 2017: 224–225.

The constitutional amendment that abolished the Individual Voters' seats, passed in 2014, was seen as tidying up a 'temporary ruling' that was made 54 years previously during the 1960 Constitutional Convention to provide representation for European voters. At that time it was considered that the distinction between 'European' and 'Sāmoan' would fade over time. This proved to be the case and the amendment formalised this fact.

The naming of the role and the formal address in Sāmoan language of the Head of State of the Independent State of Sāmoa, *'O le Ao o le Mālō o Mālō Sa'oloto Tūto'atasi o Sāmoa,* has led to some tension. In Sāmoan *Susuga* is a style of address that translates as 'Your Honour' or 'Your Excellency' in English; and *Afioga* also translates as 'Your Honour' or 'Your Excellency'. Malietoa Tanumafili II, as Head of State, always insisted on being addressed as *Susuga.* The next Head of State, Tui Atua Tupua Tamasese Efi, insisted on being addressed in English as 'Your Royal Highness'. The constitutional amendment that confirmed the formal title as *'O le Ao o le Mālō* gives precedence to the Sāmoan indigenous language, steering the term of address away from the European concept of royalty.

In 2020–21 Tuila'epa introduced, and Parliament passed, further constitutional amendments primarily focused on the Land and Titles Court and designed to correct an historical anomaly. These amendments were subject to significant public debate and consultation before they were passed into law. It is useful to consider the history and reasoning behind these changes.

In 1900, Dr Wilhelm Solf, the Governor of German Sāmoa, imported the German Imperial legal system into Sāmoa, headed by an Imperial Judge. He also established a 'native' administration, including a system of courts to deal with Sāmoan offenders, appointing loyal supporters as *Fa'amasino Sili* (Sāmoan Chief Judge), subordinate to the Imperial Judge, and as *Fa'amasino Itūmālō* (District Judges). In 1903, a Land and Titles Commission, staffed by Europeans, was established to hear and decide on disputes over land and *matai* titles. Today's Land and Titles Court (LTC) is a direct descendant of the German Commission, but the LTC is now fully staffed by Sāmoans. Since independence the number of legally trained and qualified lawyers has increased and there has been a policy of 'Sāmoanisation' of the judiciary.

Since independence, 'Sāmoa has sought to build a legal system that supports the modern ideal of democracy without significantly compromising its cultural heritage and uniqueness'.[3] There is an inbuilt tension between Sāmoan customary law, which 'developed as a means to defend and protect the group' (family, village) and 'uphold the authority of *matai*', and a legal system that 'is based on principles of individual rights'. In Sāmoa, the Judges of the Supreme and Magistrate's Courts deal with criminal offences and civil matters and the *Fa'amasino Sāmoa* of the Land and Titles Court deal with matters relating to disputes over customary lands and titles.

Former Chief Justice, Patu Sapolu, used the term 'Legal Pluralism' to refer to a country with two legal systems.[4] In most circumstances these two systems run in parallel with few problems. However, matters in the Land and Titles Court that are taken to appeal are dealt with by the Chief Justice and the Supreme Court, or the Court of Appeal, which leads to difficulties as judges of these two courts do not necessarily have the cultural and language skills to deal with the nuances of judgements regarding *matai* titles and customary land issues. It was these matters that led to Prime Minister Tuila'epa tabling the Constitutional Amendment Bill 2020, The Lands and Titles Bill 2020 and the Judicature Bill 2020. One effect of these bills was to remove the subordinate position of the Land and Titles Court. Significant debate and controversy followed.[5]

A Parliamentary Select Committee, chaired by Gatoloaifaana Amata Alesana-Gidlow, undertook a wide six-month consultation process, travelling throughout Savai'i and 'Upolu to conduct village meetings to explain, discuss and receive feedback on the proposed

3   See Sapolu, P. et al., 2012: 18.
4   Comments to Special Parliamentary Committee, 12 May 2020. Reported in *Sāmoa Observer*.
5   See *Sāmoa Observer* Online from March, 2020 for comments from both sides of the debate including: the Sāmoa Law Society; Former Judge Lefau Harry Schuster; Matāutu Village; Former Head of State Tui Atua Tupua Tamasese Efi and Amnesty International.

legislation. In July 2020, part way through the consultation process, Gatoloaifaana reported that, '. . . there were villages that expressed opposition due to some statements which had been made by those who went there before us, but with the rest of the villages, after the Parliamentary Committee had explained where the bills came from and how they came about, they understood and gave their support.' Gatoloaifaana noted that '. . . the most concerning provision of the bills is the proposed change in the limits to the number of *matai sa'o* a family can have to just five . . .'[6]

The Constitutional Amendment Bill 2020, The Lands and Titles Bill 2020 and The Judicature Bill 2020 were passed into law. However, the passing of the laws by a 46 to 4 majority did not end the public debate but led to a political crisis. Fiamē Naomi Matā'afa voted against the bills and resigned as Deputy Prime Minister, citing the passing of the new laws as the reason for her move, and shortly joined forces with Laauli Leuatea Schmidt who had established the FAST Party following his sacking from HRPP. The final result of the 2021 General Election led to Fiamē Naomi Matā'afa becoming Prime Minister of a FAST Government. A two-thirds majority in a parliamentary vote is required to overturn constitutional amendments or pass new amendments.

6 *Sāmoa Observer* Online, 28 July, 2020.

Appendix 3

Women's Representation[1]

The 10% minimum requirement, for seats to increase women's participation in Parliament, was prompted by the United Nations Secretary General Ban Ki Moon who noted at the 2011 FORUM meeting in New Zealand that nine countries in the Commonwealth had either no female representatives or were under-represented in their parliaments. Six of these were Pacific Island nations, including Sāmoa.

In 2013, the HRPP Government introduced an amendment to Article 44 of the Constitution that requires a minimum of 10% female Members of Parliament, to increase women's participation in the social, economic and political development of Sāmoa. If less than 10% are elected through the ballot on a General Election, further women may be appointed to make up the full 10%.

The 2016 General Election was the first time that the new amendment was put into effect. Mrs Faaulusau Rosa, from Gagaemauga No. 3, won the fifth seat to make up the full 10% requirement. This raised the total number of seats in Parliament from 49 to 50. Further electoral reforms raised the number of seat to 51. The application of the minimum women's representation after the 2021 General Election added another seat for women taking the total seats to 52, including six female representatives.

The calculation of the 10% is straightforward. Selection is based on the women that polled the highest votes expressed as a percentage of the individual members' electoral roll. In this way all female candidates from large and small electorates have an equal chance of selection. Hon. Fiamē Naomi Matā'afa was Minister in Charge

1 This note is based, in part, on Tuila'epa Sa'ilele Malielegaoi's Address to the Nation delivered on 23 May, 2021 in which he explained the Constitutional Amendment to Article 44.

of both Electoral Matters and the Justice Ministry responsible for implementing the amendments from 2011 to 2016.

Former Chief Justice Patu noted, in an interview on TV1 on Saturday 29 May 2021, that

> The current number of 5 elected women MPs amounts to only 9.8% of women MPs and does not meet the Constitutional requirement of 10% minimum. In the circumstances the Head of State cannot lawfully convene the Legislative Assembly until the Constitutional requirement for women is met or the Court of Appeal makes a decision through due process. This explains the suspension on 22 May 2021 by the Head of State of an earlier proclamation on 20 May for the convening of Parliament on Monday 24 May 2021.

This suspension proclamation by the Head of State was duly cancelled by the court ruling on Pentecost Sunday, which led to the tent swearing-in ceremony on 24 May. This was later declared illegal and unconstitutional by the Supreme Court on 20 June 2021, but later made legal again by the Appeal Court decision on 23 July 2021.

Appendix 4

Harmony Agreement

The Harmony Agreement, as outlined in the Supreme Court's verdict on the Contempt of Court case against Tuila'epa Dr Sa'ilele Malielegaoi and other HRPP members, reads:

The Hon Fiame Matā'afa MP, in her own capacity and as leader of Fa'atuatua i Le Atua Samoa Ua Tasi and the Hon Tuila'epa Sa'ilele Malielegaoi MP, in his own capacity and as leader of the Human Rights Protection Party have agreed, with the permission of the Supreme Court, to discontinue the contempt proceedings between them.

The two Hon Leaders have engaged in thorough discussion following the aftermath of the April 2021 General Election and the consequent court proceedings and the wider challenges that Samoa now faces.

They have formed the common view that it is now necessary: to ensure and secure political and social stability for the benefit of all people and residents of Samoa;

To promote peace and harmony for the public of Samoa, which is the prevailing public interest in light of the months of uncertainty and disruption to the conduct of governance after the general elections in April 2021;

To face the current challenges to Samoa in terms of the global pandemic brought upon by Covid-19 and the effect on the environment caused by climate change, as a nation united under God; and

To recognise that Samoa is a small country with limited resources and therefore particularly vulnerable during times of economic, political and social instability and, further, that Samoa has a unique culture where everyone is connected one way or another either through family ties or *matai* titles;

To restore public confidence in all the democratic institutions upon which our government and society are founded;

To restore and acknowledge the traditional honour and dignity belonging to all those who lead the country, from the heart of each family, to the villages, districts and islands; and in doing so seek to respect the overarching spiritual leadership of the various denominations of our Christian churches for the glory of God.

They have, therefore, agreed that, rather than cause further disagreement and disharmony, they discontinue the contempt proceedings and, further: to emphasise and uphold their shared respect, and their support for all Samoa to respect, for the Supreme Court, the Court of Appeal and the judiciary of Samoa; and to record their agreement to move forward under the Constitution, with which Samoa is blessed and under which the courts of Samoa were able to resolve the unprecedented disagreements of the past year.[1]

---

1   The Harmony Agreement did not last. On 24 May 2022, the Parliamentary Privileges and Ethics Committee recommended to the Legislative Assembly that Opposition Leader, Tuila'epa Sa'lele Malielegaoi and Party Secretary, Lealailepule Rimoni Aiafi, be suspended from Parliament indefinitely without pay and parliamentary allowances, for contempt of Parliament in their comments following the 2021 General Election. Members of the Opposition objected and rejected the findings of the FAST-dominated Committee to no avail.

Bibliography

Aikman, Colin. 2000, 2010. 'Powles, Guy Richardson', *Dictionary of New Zealand Biography. Te Ara – The Encyclopedia of New Zealand,* teara.govt.nz/en/biographies/5p37/powles-guy-richardson

Baker, P. and Glasser, S. 2020. *The Man Who Ran Washington – The Life and Times of James A. Baker III.* New York: Doubleday.

Brunt, T. 2016. *To Walk Under Palm Trees, The Germans in Sāmoa: Snapshots from Albums – Part 1.* Apia: Sāmoa Historical and Cultural Trust.

Buzacott, A. 1866 (1985 Reprint). *Mission Life in the Islands of the Pacific,* London: John Snow & Co., Reprinted by University of the South Pacific, Suva.

Campbell, I. 1991. *A History of the Pacific Islands.* Christchurch: Canterbury University Press.

Churchward, W. 1887 (1971 reprint). *My Consulate in Sāmoa – A record of four years sojourn in the Navigators Islands, with personal experiences of King Malietoa Laupepa, his country and his men.* London: Dawsons.

Crocombe, R. and A. Ali, 1983. *Politics in Polynesia,* Suva: University of the South Pacific.

Crowe, A. 2018. *Pathway of the Birds: The Voyaging Achievements of Maori and Their Polynesian Ancestors.* Auckland: Bateman.

Dalrymple, W. 2019. *The Anarchy – The Relentless Rise of the East India Company.* London: Bloomsbury

Davidson, J. 1967. *Samoa Mo Samoa: The Emergence of the Independent State of Western Samoa.* Melbourne: Oxford University Press.

Davies, N. 2018. *Beneath Another Sky: A Global Journey into History.* London: Penguin Press.

Field, M. 1984. *Mau: Sāmoa's Struggle Against New Zealand Oppression,*

Wellington: A.H. & A. W. Reed Ltd.

Field, M. 2006. *Black Saturday: New Zealand's Tragic Blunders in Sāmoa*. Wellington: Reed Books.

Field, M. 2010. *Swimming with Sharks – Tales from the Pacific Frontline*. Auckland: Penguin Books.

Firth, S. (ed.), 2006. *Globalisation and Governance in the Pacific Islands*. Canberra, ANU E Press.

Fukuyama, F. 2011. *The Origins of Political Order – From Prehuman Times to the French Revolution*. London: Profile Books.

Fukuyama, F. 2014. *Political Order and Political Decay – From the Industrial Revolution to the Globalisation of Democracy*. London: Profile Books.

Fukuyama, F. 2018. *Identity – The Demand for Dignity and the Politics of Resentment*. London: Profile Books.

Gilson. R. 1970. *Sāmoa 1830 to 1900: The Politics of a Multi-Cultural Community*. Melbourne: Oxford University Press.

Gonthier, de P. 1997 . . . *a-t-on des Nouvelles de Monsieur de Laperouse? recit d'une expedition*. Noumea: Association Salomon Nouvelle-Caledonie.

Harris, D. et al. 2020. 'Evolutionary History of Modern Sāmoans'. *Proceedings of the National Academy of Sciences of the United States of America*. PNAS first published April 14, 2020. https://doi.org/10.1073/pnas.1913157117

Hobson, J.A. 1938. *Imperialism: A Study*. London

Hau'ofa, E. 1994. 'Our Sea of Islands' in *The Contemporary Pacific*, 6, No.1: 149–161.

Hau'ofa, E. 1998. 'The Ocean in Us' in *The Contemporary Pacific*, 10, No.2: 392–410.

Howe, K.R. (Ed.) 2006. *Vaka Moana – Voyages of the Ancestors: The Discovery and Settlement of the Pacific*. Auckland: Bateman/Auckland Museum.

Huffer, E. and So'o, A. (Eds.) 2000. *Governance in Sāmoa – Pulega i Sāmoa.* Suva: University of the South Pacific and Canberra: Asia Pacific Press.

Iati Iati, 2013. 'Sāmoa's Price for 25 Years of Political Stability', *Journal of Pacific History*, 48 (4), 2013, 443–63.

Johnstone, I. and Powles, M. (Eds.), 2012. *New Flags Flying – Pacific Leadership.* Wellington: Huia.

Keesing, F. 1934. *Modern Sāmoa – Its Government and Changing Life.* London: Allen and Unwin.

Kramer, A. 1994. *The Sāmoa Islands Volume I.* Translated by T. Verhaaren. Auckland: Polynesian Press.

Kramer, A. 1994. *The Sāmoa Islands Volume II.* Translated by T. Verhaaren. Auckland: Polynesian Press.

Laracy, H. 1998. 'Nelson, Olaf Frederick' in *Dictionary of New Zealand Biography.* https://teara.govt.nz/en/biographies/4n5/nelson-olaf-Frederick (accessed 14 May 2019).

Levine, S. (Ed.) 2009. *Pacific Ways: Government and Politics in the Pacific Islands.* Wellington: Victoria University Press.

Lewis, D. 1994. *We, the Navigators: The Ancient Art of Landfinding in the Pacific,* Second Edition. Honolulu: University of Hawaii Press.

London Missionary Society, 1958. *'O le Tusi Faalupega o Sāmoa.* Mālua: LMS Press.

Malielegaoi, T. 2016a. *Saunoaga a le Afioga a le Palemia.* Tatalaina Polokalame Faamasani mo Sui Usufono o le Palemene Lona XVI. 15 Mati 2016.

Malielegaoi, T. 2016b. *Presentation 1. System of Government: The Sāmoan Arrangement.* Folasaga 1. Afioga i le Palemia, Faataatiaga o le Faiga-Mālō a Sāmoa. 29 Mati 2016.

Malielegaoi, T. 2016c. *Presentation 2 HRPP Longevity: Political, Economic and Social Implications.* Saunoaga a le Afioga i le Palemia. Fonotaga Faale-Aoaoga mo Sui Usufono o le Palemene Lona XVI. 29

Mati 2016.

Malielegaoi, T. 2016d. *Parliamentarians: Varied Expectations and Leadership Qualities.* Saunoaga a le Afioga i le Palemia. Fonotaga Faale-Aoaoga mo Sui Usufono o le Palemene Lona XVI. 30 Mati 2016.

Malielegaoi, T. and P. Swain, 2017. *Pālemia: Prime Minister Tuilaʻepa Saʻilele of Sāmoa – A Memoir.* Wellington: Victoria University Press.

Malielegaoi, T., P. Swain, 2021. *Pālemia - Tuilaʻepa Saʻilele Pālemia o le Mālō o Sāmoa.* Ueligitone: Lōmia e le Iunivesitē of Vitoria i Ueligitone.

Malielegaoi, T. 2020. Address by the Hon. Prime Minister Tuilaʻepa Sai'lele Malielegaoi to the QS Global Focus Summit. Victoria University of Wellington, 21 February 2020.

Malielegaoi, T. 2021. *My Response to the Joint Communication of the Office of the High Commissioner of the Unieted Nations Human Rights.* Apia: 30 September 2021. (See full text in Appendix 3.)

Mālō O Sāmoa. 1960. *Lipoti Faamaonia O Felafolafoaiga O Le Fono Faavae A Sāmoa, Tusi I, II, III, [I Le Gagana Sāmoa].* 'Ofisa O Le Failautusi, Fono Aoao Faitulafono. Mulinuu: Sāmoa.

McGibbon, I. 1996. Richardson, George Spafford in *Dictionary of New Zealand Biography.* teara.govt.nz/en/biographies/rr16/richardson-george-spafford (accessed 24 May 2019)

Martin, J. 1991 (first published in 1817). *Tonga Islands - William Mariner's Account.* Tonga: Vavaʻu Press

Maude, H.E. 1968. *Of Islands and Men: Studies in Pacific History.* Melbourne: Oxford University Press.

Maude, H.E. 1981. *Slavers in Paradise: The Peruvian Labour Trade in Polynesia, 1862–1864.* Canberra: Australian National University Press.

Meleisea, M. 1980. *'O Tama Uli: Melanesians in Sāmoa.* Suva: University of the South Pacific.

Meleisea, M. and P. Schoeffel. 'Western Sāmoa: Like a Slippery Fish', in Crocombe, R. and A. Ali (Eds). 1983. *Politics in Polynesia*. Suva: University of the South Pacific.

Meleisea, M. 1987. *The Making of Modern Sāmoa*. Suva: Institute of Pacific Studies, University of the South Pacific.

Meleisea, M. and P. Schoeffel, (Eds). 1987. *Lagaga: A Short History of Western Sāmoa*. Suva: University of the South Pacific.

Meleisea, M. 1992. *Change and Adaptions in Western Sāmoa*. Christchurch: Macmillan Brown Centre for Pacific Studies.

Meleisea, M. 1995. '"To whom the gods and men crowned": Chieftainship and Hierarchy in Ancient Sāmoa', in Huntsman, J. (Ed.). *Tonga and Sāmoa: Images of Gender and Polity*. Christchurch: Macmillan Brown Centre for Pacific Studies.

Meleisea, M., Meleisea, E. and P. Schoeffel (Eds). 2012. *Sāmoa's Journey 1962–2012, Aspects of History*. Wellington: Victoria University Press.

Meleisea, M. and P. Schoeffel. 2015. 'Land, Custom and History in Sāmoa' in *The Journal of Sāmoan Studies*, Vol. 5: 23–39. Apia: Centre for Sāmoan Studies, National University of Sāmoa.

Melville, H. 1846. *Typee – A Peep at Polynesian Life*. London: John Murray.

Melville, H. 1847. *Omoo - A Narrative of Adventures in the South Seas*. London: John Murray.

Meti, L. 2002. *Sāmoa: The Making of the Constitution*. Lepapaigalagala, Sāmoa: National University of Sāmoa.

Milner, G. 1976. *Sāmoan Dictionary*. London: Oxford University Press.

Moors, H. 1926 (1986 reprint). *Some Recollections of Early Sāmoa*. Apia: The Western Sāmoa Historical and Cultural Trust.

Munro, D. 1996. 'Robert Logan' in *Dictionary of New Zealand Biography*. teara.govt.nz/en/biographies/3l12/logan-robert (accessed 23 May 2019).

O'Brien, P. 2017. *Tautai, Sāmoa, World History & the Life of Taʻisi O. F. Nelson*. Wellington: Huia.

Osterhammel, J. 2005. *Colonisation: A Theoretical Overview*. Princeton: Princeton University Press.

Pacific Islands Forum Secretariat. 2014. *The Framework for Pacific Regionalism*. Suva: PIFS.

Powles, M. (ed.), 2016. *China and the Pacific: The View from Oceania*. Wellington, Victoria University Press.

Pratt, G. 1977. *Pratt's Grammar and Dictionary of the Sāmoan Language*. Apia: Mālua Printing Press.

Report of the Royal Commission concerning the Administration of Western Sāmoa. 1927. AJHR (Appendix to the Journals of the House of Representatives of New Zealand), 1928, A4b.

Richards, R. 2017. *Bold Captains: Trans-Pacific Exploration and Trade 1780–1830, Volumes 1 & 2*. Porirua: Paremata Press.

Rigby, N., Van Der Merwe, P. and Williams, G. 2018. *Pacific Exploration: Voyages of Discovery from Cook's Endeavour to the Beagle*. London: Adlard Coles.

Salesa, D. 'The Pacific in Indigenous Time', in Armitage, D. & Bashford, A (eds.) 2016, *Pacific Histories: Ocean, Land, People*. Basingstoke: Palgrave Macmillan.

Salesa, D. 2017. *Island Times – New Zealand's Pacific Futures*. Wellington: Bridget Williams Books.

Salesa, D. 'Native Seas and Native Seaways: The Pacific Ocean and New Zealand', in Steel, F. (ed.) 2018, *New Zealand and the Sea: Historical Perspectives*. Wellington: Bridget Williams Books.

Sapolu, P. et al. 'Law and Custom' in Meleisea, M., Meleisea, E. and P. Schoeffel (Eds). 2012. *Sāmoa's Journey 1962–2012: Aspects of History*. Wellington: Victoria University Press.

Shaffer, R. 2011. *Sāmoa, A Historical Novel*. San Diego: Centennial Books.

Smith, A. 1759. *The Theory of Moral Sentiments*. London: Millar.

So'o, A. 2006. 'More than 20 years of political stability in Sāmoa under the Human Rights Protection Party', in Firth, S. (ed.) *Globalisation and Governance in the Pacific Islands*. Canberra: ANU E Press: 350–351.

So'o, A. et al. (Eds). 2006. *Sāmoa National Human Development Report, Sustainable Livelihoods in a Changing Sāmoa*. Apia: Centre for Sāmoan Studies, National University of Sāmoa.

So'o, A. (Ed.). 2007. *Changes in the Matai System – 'O Suiga i le Fa'amatai*. Apia: Centre for Sāmoan Studies, National University of Sāmoa.

So'o, A. 2008. *Democracy and Custom in Sāmoa: An Uneasy Alliance*. Suva: IPS Publications, University of the South Pacific.

So'o, A. 2009. 'Sāmoa' in Levine, S. (Ed.). *Pacific Ways: Government and Politics in the Pacific Islands*. Wellington: Victoria University Press.

So'o, A. 'Political Development: Sāmoa's Parliamentary Journey from 1962 to 2012', in Meleisea M. et al. (Eds.). 2012. *Sāmoa's Journey 1962–2012: Aspects of History*. Wellington: Victoria University Press.

Stevenson, R.L. 1892 (reprinted 1967). *A Footnote to History: Eight Years of Trouble in Sāmoa*. London: Dawsons of Pall Mall.

Sumption, J. 2019. *In Praise of Politics*, Second Reith Lecture. London: BBC. https://www.bbc.co.uk/programmes/m0005f05

Swain, P. 1999. *Civil Society and Development: Pacific Island Case Studies*, PhD dissertation, Massey University.

Swain, P. 2014. 'Fitting into the Pacific', in J. Schultz and L. Jones (eds.), *Pacific Highways, Griffith Review 43*, Brisbane: Griffith University.

Tabangcora, B. 'An Analysis of the 2021 Electoral Decisions of the Sāmoan Courts', in *Comparative Law Journal of the Pacific*, Vol. 26, 2021: 107–124.

Techerkézoff, S. 2008. *First Contacts in Polynesia: The Sāmoan Case (1722–1848) Western Misunderstandings about Sexuality and Divinity.* Canberra: ANU Press.

Thode-Arora, H. (Ed.). 2014. *From Sāmoa with Love? Sāmoan Travellers in Germany 1895–1911, Tracing the Footsteps.* Munich: Hirmer Verlag.

Thomas, N. 2004. *Discoveries, The Voyages of Captain Cook.* London: Penguin Books.

Toleafoa, A. 2013. 'One Party State: The Sāmoan Experience', in D. Hegarty and D. Tryon (eds), *Politics, Development and Security in Oceania,* Canberra: ANU-E Press.

Truman, H. 1949. *Inaugural Address of Harry S. Truman, January 20 1949.* https://avalon.law.yale.edu/20th_century/truman.asp

Tuimaleali'ifano, A.M. 2006. *'O Tama-a-'Āiga: The Politics of Succession to Sāmoa's Paramount Titles,* Suva: University of the South Pacific.

Turner, G. 1884 (reprinted 1984). *Sāmoa: A Hundred Years Ago and Long Before.* Suva: University of the South Pacific.

Ulu, A.J. 2013. *Pule: Development Policy Sovereignty in Sāmoa,* Masters in Development Studies thesis, Victoria University of Wellington.

United Nations, 2021. *Report of United Nations Human Rights Special Rapporteurs on the independence of judges and lawyers and the Working Group on the discrimination against women and girls.* Ref: AL WSM 1/2021. Geneva, United Nations. 4 August 2021.

Va'a, F.P.S., T.U. Va'a, F.L. Fuata'i, M.I. Chan Mow and D. Amosa, 2012. 'Aspects of Economic Development', in M. Meleisea et al. (eds), *Sāmoa's Journey 1962–2012: Aspects of History,* Wellington: Victoria University Press.

Wendt, A. 1965. *Guardians and Wards – A study of the origins, causes and the first two years of the Mau in Western Sāmoa.* Masters thesis, Victoria University of Wellington.

Index

Batavia, 32
Becker, Herr, 63
Behrens, Karl Friedrich, 32
Belgian Congo, 99
Bell, Gertrude, 101
Berlin Conference, 65, 68
Betham, George, 103–104, 114
Betham-Savalenoa, Savalenoa Mareva, 128, 130, 133–134
Bethune, Captain Charles, 43
Bismarck, Herbert von, 65
Bismark, 60
Black Saturday, 93–95
'blackbirding', 36
Botany Bay, 34
Bouman (Baumann), Cornelis, 32
Bounty mutineers, 34
Boussole, 33
Braisby, A.L., 95
Brandeis, Eugen, 63–65
bribery, 130
Budget, 121, 132–134
Buzacott, Aaron, 38(n19)
by-elections, 121, 130–131, 134(n52), 136(n57), 137

C
Cabinet, 104–105, 109, 114, 118, 120–122, 133, 146
California, 33
Cambridge University, 92
Cape Horn, 33
Caretaker Prime Minister, 125–128
Caribbean, 101
Caroline Islands, 24
Cathedral of Immaculate Conception, 129
Cedercrantz, Otto, 65
Central Polynesian Land and Commercial Company (CPLCC), 58
Chambers, William, 68–69
Chauvel, M., 42, 46–47
Chief Justice, 65–66, 68–69, 79, 128,

142, 149, 152
Chief Justice (NZ), 90
Chile, 32, 33, 99
China, 62, 74, 82, 82(n4), 96
Christian Laws, code of, 37
Church of Jesus Christ of Latter-Day Saints, 38, 42–43
Citizens Committee, 86, 89–91
citizenship, 109
Citizenship of Western Sāmoa Bill, 109
civil administration, New Zealand, 85
civil disobedience campaign, 90–91
civil war, 39–40, 48, 50, 54–58, 61, 69, 114. *See also* warfare
climate change, 138, 153
Coates, Gordon, 89, 92
Cobbe, John George, 94
cocoa, 74, 82, 97
coconut oil, 46–48, 57, 59, 62, 74
Coe, Jonas, 54
colonisation, definition, 72–73
commissions of inquiry, 120
common status, 105
communalism, 17(n2)
Condominium, 65–66
Congregational Christian Church of Sāmoa, 40
consensus politics, 118–119, 126, 129
constituencies, 105, 107, 121
Constitution, Draft, 108–112
Constitution of the Independent State of Samoa, 38, 99(n18), 112–113, 129, 131, 133. *See also* Appendix 2
Constitutional Amendment Bill 2020, 149–150
constitutional amendments, 124, 140, 142. *See also* Appendix 2; Appendix 3
constitutional changes, 100
Constitutional Convention (1954), 104–107, 112
Constitutional Convention (1960), 108, 110, 112–114, 148